MW01255106

Retiring Minds

Life after Work

Collected and Edited by

Susan Thurin

Copyright © 2008 by Susan Thurin

ISBN 0-7414-4366-X

After first publication, rights revert to the individual authors.

Cover photo "Bird" is by Robert Meier.

Published by:

INFIꝏITY
PUBLISHING.COM

1094 New DeHaven Street, Suite 100
West Conshohocken, PA 19428-2713
Info@buybooksontheweb.com
www.buybooksontheweb.com
Toll-free (877) BUY BOOK
Local Phone (610) 941-9999
Fax (610) 941-9959

Printed in the United States of America

Printed on Recycled Paper

Published January 2008

Grateful acknowledgment is made to the following for permission to reprint previously published material:

James Eggert's "What's Wrong with Capitalism—A Prairie's Perspective" is reprinted in modified form from *Wonder of the Tao: A Meditation on Spirituality and Ecological Balance* (Atlanta & Fort Worth: Humanics Publishing Group, 2004), Ch. 3.

Robert Meier's photos illustrating "Retired Buildings" were printed in color in *Architecture Minnesota*, July-August 2005, pp. 49-53.

Darshan Perusek's "Another Bend in the River" is an excerpt from "Shades of Autumn: Reflections on the Threshold of the Retired Life" in *South Asian Review* (Vol. 27, No. 3) 2006.

Patricia Zontelli's "Night Swim," "Small Lake Up North," "Still Center," and "Loss" were first published in *Red Cross Dog*, New Rivers Press, 2000. Copyright 2000 by Patricia Zontelli. Reprinted by permission of the author and New Rivers Press.

For all those who have gone before us

Contents

Work without Borders

Women Academics, Women's Roles

Acknowledgments

I am grateful to the contributors for their willingness to tell their stories with verve. They have been a source of encouragement, their stories a delight. Special thanks are due to Emily Meier for her close reading and editing of several of the essays included here. Her writerly advice is always wise. Mim Canny and David McCordick evaluated several essays and offered good advice on the manuscript. Many thanks to Robert Meier for the splendid cover art provided for this book. Sigrid Thurin, Annette Taylor and Denise Sedlak were a helpful focus group. Thanks to all those who offered alternative titles; I hope I chose the right one. Finally, the support of family and friends, especially Judy O'Connor-Schremp, has helped me see this project through.

Susan Thurin

The Way Out, an Introduction

Many retirees can identify with Professor Job who told me that his adjustment to retirement spanned the time it took him to leave his desk for the last time and to reach his car in the parking lot. Job's experience isn't universal, however. For retirees from every kind of work—even some big lottery winners say they want to return to work as usual—just thinking about retirement is cause for alarm. In fact, the word retirement itself is so fraught with conflicted feelings that friends cautioned against using it even in a subtitle for this book. "It's too negative; defer any mention of it to the back cover," one person offered. "But the book *is* about retirement," I insisted, "Why try to hide it? It's something to embrace." What starts in anxiety for some people evolves into blissful leisure, a time to start a new sort of life, a time to fill in what was missed during the work years. It's a good time in life. To recognize that fact, this volume aims both to celebrate what people do after the career years and to honor the inevitabilities that ensue.

I first thought of retirement at age twenty-six during my first year as a college teacher. The retirement I contemplated was not my own but that of Lois and Karen, middle-aged professors whom I imagined were on the threshold of retirement, for to my youthful eyes, they represented an obsolete role model rather than pre-Betty Freidan feminism. When years later both retired, they redefined themselves, Lois becoming the resident humanist in her old hometown, Karen an opera buff. Another colleague, Morrell, a popular technical writing professor who loved jokes, often laughed that he would retire at sixty-five unless he got senile, in which case he'd "stay until seventy, like the rest of them." Many colleagues took retirement as a departure, moving out west or down south, and a few retired with a hang-dog attitude, ending their professional life with a sense of disappointment and bitterness.

From the printed page come other examples of leaving the work world behind. Carl Klaus, a highly successful professor who headed the writing program at the University of Iowa, is strung out with worry as he plans his retirement, according to the story he tells in *Taking Retirement: A Beginner's Diary*. He obsesses about continuing to have a university office, for he still has several publishing commitments and graduate students to direct at the time of his retirement. "What is he complaining about?" I ask myself. It doesn't sound as if he is retiring at all, other than giving up a seminar and paper grading; however, by the end of his book, he questions his months of hand-wringing. As his professional responsibilities recede into the background, he relishes the freedom of his retired life and wonders why he had approached it with so much apprehension.

In contrast, Carolyn Heilbrun finds retirement exhilarating release. After a stunning career, she confesses in *The Last Gift of Time: Life Beyond Sixty*, "I was shocked, almost from the moment I left Columbia, by how little I missed it, how relieved I was not to have to plunge, ever again, into that poisonous atmosphere" (NY: The Dial Press, 1997, p. 39). A little later she adds: "I entered upon a life unimagined previously, of happiness impossible to youth or to the years of being constantly needed both at home and at work. I entered into a period of freedom . . . to live without a constant, unnoticed stream of anger and resentment, without the daily contemplation of power always in the hands of the least worthy, the least imaginative, the least generous." If one wore one's work life as a poisonous necklace, getting rid of it would be a relief, no doubt about it. For most academics, though, the necklace is beaded with a satisfying combination of teaching, writing, and university service textured by department politics and collegial banter, a career built around students, the young minds waiting to be informed, the captive audience on which to drop pearls of wisdom.

Still, when my turn came to retire, I found these various exit-models of only modest help, for deprived of teaching and other responsibilities that defined me professionally, what would be left? Those hard-won curriculum vitae items under "Publications and Presentations," now moldering away on a library shelf, or stored even more invisibly on the internet, or simply forgotten, seemed increasingly irrelevant. Retirement meant the loss of a title that indicated how I earned a living. It meant an identity change, akin to taking my husband's surname at marriage and becoming someone new.

To add to my confusion, my sister Fran was disappointed when I told her about my plan to retire. She knew I liked my job and she worried about me not having much to do when I stopped working. I'm sure we both had our parents in mind. Our father's dream was to leave the Minnesota farm and live in a cabin up north. "Up north?" mother cried, "We *are* north!" Mother's fear of that retirement was sadly unnecessary, for she died just before her sixty-fifth birthday, and though my favorite picture of my father shows him slightly stooped as he carries his fishing gear, he's leaving the dock on our lake, not one farther north. In our parents' world, retirement was essentially theoretical. Perhaps Fran, on some level, felt that a "modern" retirement for us or any of our siblings would be yet another way in which we vaulted over the hard realities of our parents' lives.

As uneasy as it made me, I knew I had to follow through on my plan. Feeling adrift in uncharted waters in the first months after ending my university career, I searched for ways to put so much unstructured time to use. This general distress soon gave way to the specific when I learned that my husband Erik's prostate cancer had metastasized to the bones and that his life expectancy was one to two years, "maybe less," the doctor added ominously. It's a message that summons all the clichés. You gulp, your shoulders droop, you stumble out of the clinic. Erik and I knew that his health was deteriorating, for that was one of the considerations in the timing of my retirement, but a certain prognosis is different from a gradual decline. We continued our usual activities as best we could for as long as we could, Erik fiddling with his journals, I seizing on the idea of recruiting friends and former colleagues to write about their experience of retirement for this wide-ranging volume.

Though the project was born of desperation, it developed a happy life of its own. Some authors signed on with enthusiasm, some with reluctance, and all have found retirement a spur to their creative impulse. The original idea was to be lighthearted, retired professors telling amusing stories about their current lives. Several contributors have taken that approach, but retirees tend to be reflective, and so their stories vary in mood and form. The reader will find mostly essays here but also poetry and clever pieces of memoiristic fiction.

To begin, there are four ways of addressing Retirement Angst, four ways of answering the frequent question, "Do retirees have any regrets about their new life?" Richard Gardner's "A Fool's Leviathan," a story about the decision to retire, evokes the sensations of a drowning man whose life flashes by him, only to be happily rescued. Next, Sudershan Perusek recounts her first day of retirement and the unfolding of her new life with an appeal to Indian philosophy in "Another Bend in the River." Then, with high-spirited musings, William O'Neill dismisses the vicissitudes of retirement by relishing a sort of second adolescence as an opportunity for whimsy and dodging moralizing about time and purpose. The section ends on a more serious note with Patricia Zontelli's poems that probe memory and growing old. Using imagery drawn from the natural world, the poems make the familiar shimmer with comfort and tranquility.

The other sections of Retiring Minds describe numerous activities and approaches to life during retirement. Since reading and writing were essential to their work, many academics luxuriate in re-defining these lifelong interests. The Writing after Work section begins with Gene Bloedorn illustrating this in deed as well as in word: he is using his retirement from being a professor of art to write short stories about a long-married retired couple. His "Life with a Cat" examines the way memories cause confusion and disorientation in the "new middle age." In "To Dance in Forbidden Fields," James Eggert finds in retirement an opportunity to combine his professional interest in economics with a personal interest in ecology and spirituality. Next, Jared Brown describes the process of settling on writing as a retirement occupation after a period of fretfulness about what to do with his new freedom from work. Plans are all well and good, but they don't always work out, and Brown insists that creative laissez-faire-ness provides a happy substitute. The Writing after Work section concludes with selections from the journals of Erik Thurin illustrating his favored activities of reading and writing, his bons mots, and thoughts about mortality.

It would be remiss to have a collection about the experience of retirement without acknowledging the effects of time rolling on. The Maturing Things section pays homage to this with both professional interest and jocularity. To begin, Robert Meier discusses his photography in a striking photo essay about retired buildings in Minneapolis and St. Paul. Next, Richard Beckham approaches the subject of aging with bravado in his humorous commentary on "geriatria," places where elderly people congregate. Carol Dolphin's poem "Monochromatic Prism" takes an inspired approach in seeing the "new grayness" as a symbol of moderation. The section is completed with David McCordick's hilarious though sobering health care story.

Next we turn to travel, one of the favored activities of retirees. As the growth of the cruise industry, elderhostels, and snowbirding attest, retirees love the road, tourism, a change of scenery. The travel stories we present in this volume are set in favorite destinations of American tourists: England, Central America, and Texas. Sue Bridwell Beckham combines a recent trip to England with a retrospect on her Anglophilia and Carol Dolphin offers a picturesque view of Guatemala. Mary Thompson, joining the ranks of those who mark their retirement with a definitive change, describes her decision to pull up stakes and move cross-country.

Volunteerism, the new profession of many retirees, is addressed in the Work without Borders section. The section begins with the account of Leland Nichols who places himself in the midst of one of the greatest natural disasters in American history with his Red Cross work in New Orleans after the Hurricanes Katrina and Rita. Following the path of doing good works also, Liina Keerdoja writes about cooking for the homeless in Bethesda, Maryland. Judy Brown follows a rarer, adventurous path in using retirement to devote herself to her first love, the theater, which had been relegated to an avocational pursuit during her teaching years. Before finding rewarding new work, though, there is the letting go of a career, the subject tackled in Margaret Gordon's poem, "Flexing My Spirit Again."

The final section, titled Women Academics, Women's Roles closes the collection with writings on work and family responsibilities, the subject of much research and discussion during the feminist era which coincided with the work years of our generation. Carolyn Wedin revisits the debate about women balancing career and family, opining about the legacy of the women's movement for today's young women. For Sheri Nero and Susan Thurin, the debate about balancing career and family becomes merely academic as they are faced with traditional care giving roles and the death of a spouse. Patricia Zontelli's poem "Loss," about burying hurt, adds fitting closure to this section. In all, this volume describes retirement not as monolithic, but as varied in occupation, joy and fulfillment. Increased longevity means that most retirees have many years of this stage in their life, a long, active life after they leave their work years behind. The world is still at their feet, if they want to stoop to pick it up, or to answer the call in those prescient lines ending Alfred Lord Tennyson's poem "Ulysses":

Come, my friends,
'Tis not too late to seek a newer world.
. . . .
Tho' much is taken, much abides; and tho'
We are not now that strength which in the old days
Moved earth and heaven; that which we are, we are;
One equal-temper of heroic hearts,
Made weak by time and fate, but strong in will
To strive, to seek, to find, and not to yield.

Retirement Angst

It was the best of times, it was the worst of times. It was the age of wisdom, it was the age of foolishness . . . it was the spring of hope, it was the winter of despair, we had everything before us, we had nothing before us . . . .

Charles Dickens, *A Tale of Two Cities*

Richard Gardner

A Fool's Leviathan

Some time before grade school, Mel heard Dad say "retirement" and asked what it meant. When he gave a definition, but no example, Mel was aghast.

Already he knew his life purpose was to become an adult and pursue useful, fulfilling work. He had witnessed Dad, a natural teacher like Grandma, enlivening physics for his high school students—striding back and forth, scratching formulas on the chalk board, answering questions, calling students by name— even more rhythmically engaged and alive than he was at home.

The family hobby farm had plenty of everything—stink of privy, animal odors, smooth snakes, millions of weeds to hoe. And inside the house they were building waited Mom's books of endless words, meanings, and feelings, and family dinners, good food, and radio.

How could anyone quit all this wonder and face bare emptiness? Mel's boy-mind flashed to his time of fever, when he could not think, daydream, imagine, or enjoy anything. Did Dad mean that adulthood would come to such an end?

The horror! The horror!

So Mel grew fascinated by All and stark Nothing. A fellow kindergartner says, "I'm afraid to go to hell," and he responds, "I'm not afraid. Isn't hell better than the nothing of retirement?" The fellow can't reply. Rumors about such absurdities make Mel a wise old man beyond his years, class brain and class clown at once.

This nothing thing was too interesting to let go, and Mel found another way to use it. In learning and remembering the science and

8

literary abundance, if he quickly thought of what something was not, he had a better recall of what was. With practice he became not only the what-iffer but also the memory authority of the family, answering questions with brief factual answers that were never wrong. Meanwhile, he would notice things no one else had, simply describe them, and receive grand ooohs and aaahs. Even more, he liked to write about impossible things, pieces of nothing, that awed and mystified his classmates: "Just west of us is half a farm, and over it is half a cloud that rains half the time." Just writing this brought a little thrill, and he followed this interest into MAD parodies and science fiction. What if he just kept doing this, became a pro, and never retired?

Starting in 1805, Peter Mark Roget began "the grouping of words according to ideas" and published his first version of his Thesaurus in 1852 (xi). When Mel's family gave him a recent edition, he was awed by the thousand-or-so categories Roget used to group words, which began

> EXISTENCE
> > Being in the Abstract
> > > 1. Existence
> > > 2. Nonexistence
> > Being in the Concrete
> > > 3. Substantiality
> > > 4. Nonsubstantiality.

These categories helped organize the language of Victorian exploration and classification of biology, cultures, geology, and so forth. They also gave Mel a more complete tool for writing about both everything and nothing. To his great pleasure, he would say "Un-bad is not necessarily good," "Un-wrong is not necessarily right," "Un-logical fantasy is not necessarily bad thinking."

Soon Dad told Mel his plans: quit teaching at sixty, tend the family's five acres of avocado trees, and supplement his pension with the profits from selling the fruit.
    For a decade, about '46 to '56, he was a man of joy—up at 4:00 working on the farm, showering then leaving at 7:00 to teach, home at 4:00 to resume work before dinner—and some midnights Mel could hear him singing above the tractor roar as he cultivated

the avocado rows—working his heaven with retirement's promised land gloriously waiting.

But as Mel entered high school, Dad saw that expanding Los Angeles subdivisions would surround him, raise his taxes, and force him to sell. He sat more, learned to drink. He sold all but an acre of lawn, buildings, and trees in '58. He kept teaching well enough, and maintained his remnant of land, but became a closet alcoholic after 4:00 each day, despairing of retirement and often saying "I had a dream" (past tense).

It loomed—alcoholic un-work—leaving Mel where he started.

Mel became a victim of the not-yet-recognized disease of retirement-denial, which continued through college. Against Dad's urgings to become an engineer (like rich Uncle Leon), he majored in creative writing—surely something/nothing promised wideranging meaningful fiction.

But Mel was dogged by the family's style of memory, Dad's high-school drills in short factual answers. As Coleridge capitalized the word, Imagination "dissolves, diffuses and dissipates in order to re-create"—and Mel tried to write creatively. But Dad's style was inflexible (what was non-factual was "wrong," not creative). Mel resorted to a helpless writing from dreams as if they were facts.

A crux came at the Writer's Workshop in Iowa, where, even given plenty of time, he could not dependably generate stories—and he shifted, into literature and teaching, where an exactly compatible professor guided him to excellence.

There followed Mel's first professional year of something/ nothing, classroom/paper-grading, and giving Guidance—and he decided: "This is good enough for me."

The compatible professor recommended him for his "critical imagination"—but Mel became a graduate fellow in critical theory, where "non-logical" meant "wrong."

Yada yada—three years.

("He yada's graduate school?"

"Yes."

"I can't believe it.")

As he began his career in a family-like friendly state college, the stimulants of preps and papers kept retirement fearfully and conveniently suppressed into near-nothingness.

At this point, the gentle reader may desire to interpolate some advice, viz: "Listen here, you chucklehead. Something versus nothing hardly differs from anything is better than nothing—as if you'd be satisfied with a cave and mud bowls and grass to eat. The idea sounds powerful, but it's cruder than almost any myth. Writers choose themes to focus on—only a fool tries to write about everything."

But Mel wasn't listening—just noticed that when teaching writing and lit to so many individuals he felt comfortably disciplined—happy as a horse in the traces. As it gradually grew conscious, the theme of critical imagination, to use everywhere, brought just the right limit of freedom to both him and his students. They could close-read, generalize, articulate impressions, go off on somewhat controlled tangents—it was very versatile. The contrast with nothing made every day poignant, worthwhile, interesting, every hour and paper unique and valuable.

On a typical assignment, Mel would almost write, "Compared to nothing, this paper is quite an achievement. It has these and those good points. It can become an A if you do this and this and this and this. Why not revise and try?" Absurd and time-intensive, yes, but half the time, the strategy brought clear improvements—which, compared to nothing, was a great joy. So this nothingness was a tool, a weapon, a mental technology for career satisfaction and enjoyment.

Yet, cherished or not, the un-put-down-able priority of prep/class/grading/research demoted other pleasures to being furtive. Vacations and sabbaticals must be "productive"—how dare be "free"?

The answer was "sneakily." Over the years, All/nothing sponsored Mel's pet loves, absurdity, preposterousness, and quirky images—relief in class and outside. Secure in the traces, he reached into the nonexistent, and a joke emerged, usually unmemorable.

"We drive to distant destinations and bypass the close ones. Why not just put the short roads where the long ones are?"

"Jack Frost roasting on an open fire,
Chestnuts nipping at your nose...."

"When I come home at night late or early,
Your teeth are waiting there white and pearly...."

11

As the too-broad view invited incongruities, students said, "What?" or grinned, while friends laughed at some and tolerated the rest.

One summer in his mid-fifties, Mel had a mystic revelation—a week of internal thunder and lightning, with nameless nimbus clouds colliding like galaxies. But his notes on bits of paper added to a chaos of riddles. This All seemed too real for fiction, but trying to write it clearly brought only a stinging pain in his head. He tried for more than a year to express the experience, then—if the word may be used in retrospect—he retired from high serious-ness to scribble spoofs and humor.

Clearly, Mel's All-view, like many weapons, could dominate its wielder. In retirement's limitless freedom outside the traces, how would he find the right paths for galumphing and frolicking?

For advice, during one of their morning sessions of "tea and sympathy," Mel asked Charu, who came in her wheelchair from India at age seven.

"It's simple," she said. "Being on SSI, I have been retired most of my life. I just look and find things that are fun and do them—friends, tea-times, books on line, music, and chilling out thinking about things. But you're always worrying about getting work done—I don't know if you should retire."

"I think I could do that. But I imagine next semester and just can't push into that big black hole of retirement. Maybe I'm just in a rut."

Thanksgiving Day, on vacation with a cold, in a motel awaiting the family dinner—is this yada-nada like retirement? Half-dozing, half-idle, no urgency, a half-now with dim past and future. A kind of freedom? No special care or boredom, just not-quite-enjoying the inner/outer quiet, not really looking forward to dinner, not very enthusiastic or very sick—just low-energy.

Not "mindful," as one tradition insists. More like "void," as insists another. Or maybe just "mindless and dumb," as a colleague described a class. Or like walking in the Lake District or beside Walden Pond, waiting for inspiration—but not in the mood to ask for it. Partly, it's "just don't care, let me have this vacant peace, solitude, uninvolvement, irresponsibility."

12

Is this how great-grandpa spent his last twenty-seven years sitting watching the Pacific? A sip of wet wine, the sultry onshore breeze, crash of waves, swish of sand, stars and moon at night, and this quiet savoring of the lack of career's obligation.

Eureka! This is no "horror" of emptiness. It's like the free times I sneaked as a boy—to pretend to write, wonder about nothing, and escape from hoeing weeds or fishing in the mountains—or like the starry nights on the farm yelping back at coyotes, when it was okay to speak no words.

One afternoon over tea and crumpets, Mel talks to Amma, Charu's mom.

"It's simple," Amma says. "You just fill that emptiness with interesting things."

"No," kindergarten Mel bursts out. "It doesn't work that way. Everything is in one bag and nothing is in the other. You can't fill nothing. Nothing is just there. It's like a black hole."

Amma, like a kind mother, doesn't object—just makes that tolerating face that says, "You will think this out pretty soon."

And he does:

(- Nature abhors a vacuum.

- So do I, but look how well that horror has benefited me.

- But retirement is not The Other. It's just something to tackle like your career. You can even keep your precious nothing in the back of your mind to help enrich retirement, too.

- Duh. I should have thunk.)

To be strictly factual, deep in winter woods, not a mile from the abandoned Olson farm, wearing five layers against the twenty-below as his nose kept dripping in the wind, Mel didn't discover a large lichen-covered boulder protruding out of the snow.

On this glacial stone, in scratched rune-like letters just barely decipherable through the centuries-old weather-varnish, Mel didn't see or translate the message left for posterity.

"I, Leif Ericson," it didn't say, "have trekked here all the way from the Atlantic shores to this place to be called Wisconsin. I am forced and fated to keep exploring, even though I walk on four legs (two canes) at this evening of my life. And why? I have feared my comrades' laughing at me if I failed to die by violence and merely retired (though there is no such word yet)."

Half-astounded, Mel half-carefully considered what he had not seen, concluding, half-reasonably, that one might even retire from nonexistence, if it occurred to him to do it.

With his un-astounded half, Mel recognized thrill-chills from his childhood, which seemed too half-good in themselves to lead to anything practical.

In another stab at imagining his unknown future, Mel makes a list.
Reading? Up to a point.
Writing? Maybe.
Travel? Besides being costly, look at it. A suitcase of clothes for me, two of them for my wife Lil, and a semi full of pills.
Volunteering. Service.
Tutoring?
Coffee. Chat. Book club.
You look beforehand for that something "fulfilling" and imagination won't guarantee it.
Lil looks over his shoulder. "Doesn't the list just make things look more empty? There may be a transition, but it will be an adventure. We'll be grandparents, flea market attenders, movie viewers, helpers to friends. Even now we enjoy just sitting together with the TV off." She has this tolerating gaze like Amma's, seeing kindergarten Mel peeking through the geezer who should know better.

Not two weeks ago, Mel and Lil drove the three hours to see family in Madison, sneaking an evening with them before some teacher-union business next day. Grandson Wm (pronounced "Wm") had a cold and had missed his nap. He was quietly cranky, with short spells of crying, his world-weary eyes gazing without reaction—and Mel felt again the gray nothing-days of childhood illness. Next to Wm in the rear seat of son Ben's car en route to the restaurant and back, Mel saw Wm's eyes listlessly open and close. He did not try to stimulate Wm to perform, laugh, or smile—just touched his six-month-old hand and let Wm grasp his finger, as if for reassurance.

If Mel retired, he could do this more, when needed.

The Burger King, at mid-morning, smells of retirement. The same old men hobble in, carefully drink not too much coffee, and talk

14

about how things were—farms, trucking, sales, politics. The funeral director comes in smiling from across the street, as if jollying up future clients, though only a few laugh.

Not a week ago, Mel overheard more than enough relating to retirement. "I want something worthwhile..." "Too late now..." "I was great in those days." "My whole life..." "If only..." So much of it looked backward, as if there were no future. Or: "my back," "my cholesterol," "my heart attack"—all worries. Or: "my will," "my arrangements..."

Again Mel thought, The horror!—then recovered. How simple, he reflected; I am not they, I can do things my way for quite a while—seeing Now and Wm and Lil and tomorrow, not like a has-been, with the same joking and fun as usual. Ridiculous how hard it was to think this way: I, not someone else, will take my best tools to the future. I think I'll savor one more cup of coffee now that they all are gone.

Today, Mel's monument against "trying too hard" and "getting too serious" hangs high up his blank-white office wall. Supervising daily to-dos and goings–on, the woe-bedraggled visage (and equipage) of Don Quixote de la Mancha more-than-perceptively gazes at not only All but much of Nothing besides.

Onto Picasso's famous sketch (dusty with years) Mel long ago glued a copper-gilded feather in place of the Don's lance, evoking not even a "What?" from colleagues and students.

But now the spavined figures speak:

"Hark, Sancho," quoth the knight, "from over yon hillock I hear the fire-breathing murmur of our long-awaited foe, none other than the apocalyptic dragon Retiramente."

"Nay, sire. Methinks it is but the rustle of grass, flowers, and trees in some wind of freedom or other."

"Impossible, knave. For we have pursued this quest for 30 years, battling the intervenors of solecism, dyslogia, dyspepsia, dysfunction, and dyslexia—and no honorable god would permit a knight's ending to be so anticlimactic."

"Yada, yada, sire, yada indeed."

"Prepare my steed, my barber's basin helmet, and my trusty copper quill—and I will have at the miscreant monster with the full force of All and Nothing!"

"Be careful, master, lest thy great might turn upon thy-self."

"Stay ye back, faithful administrative assistant, while I—"

"What halts ye, sire?"

"Look and be my witness! The dragon Retiramente, out of fear of my wrath, has transformed himself into a mere lizard, a chameleon at that—blending in among the blossoms. I should have suspected—for he has such a penchant for cunning."

"Perhaps that is pension, sire."

"Begone with such quibbles, thou low-browed pragmatist! The burning question is how to joust with so minuscule an opponent."

"By all that is holy, sire, I think he has transformed himself into an un-enemy. If magic is possible, why not that?"

"You are impertinent to cajole me thus. Yet yon lizard seems to be bowing in a most conciliatory manner."

"Yes, my master," quoth the squire, "I think you need not concede to 'crass reason,' as you say, nor die of sanity as in that book about you—you need merely to live with most of your armor in storage."

A bit later today, Mel enters his office, carrying books, grade book, and Imagination. He glances up at the Knight of the Mournful Countenance, feeling whiffs of air from the Don's latest sally, or perhaps convection from the heater under the window.

Standing there a moment, still anticipating his future, he now sees two balanced options, as if shown through windows in two bags. To the right, a vista of the coming semester ranges away, hill and valley, forested by names, faces, words, and meanings. To the left, a different, similar landscape, populated by lake and meadow, already speaks to him (as ever—he should have known!) in what is also ultimately his own language.

He smiles, thinking of "Don" and "dawn"—then outright grins at how his empty fool's leviathan resolved: into a personal lizard enlivening All this, All that, and All Etc.

Another Bend in the River

It is not important at what point you stop. Stop wherever you will—only make sure that you round it off with a good ending.

Seneca

Today, as I sit at my desk to write these thoughts, is the first day of my retirement. I have been preparing myself for this day for the last two years. I've had, over this period, moments of anxiety and trepidation. I don't keep a journal, except of my insomnia, and I keep that only to remind Dr. Rosas, my doctor for the last seventeen years, that my remarkably good health not withstanding, I, too, have my share of human suffering. Those moments must have come thick and crowding as the day approached in May. I notice under the entry for March: "Two lousy nights in a row. Wide awake till four in the morning. Retirement must be weighing heavily on my mind. Made three calls yesterday about 'dark clouds and v-shaped depressions,' to quote P. G. Wodehouse, to Anne, Dave, and Leonard." I had known these moments before. There are three places where I have always felt at home: the kitchen, the garden, and the classroom. The kitchen and the garden I will have to the end of my life. The classroom had to go sometime. It was a stage where I had performed for forty years and when you are on stage, as my brother Sat says, enjoy your role and bring to it all your energy and passion. But you must also know when it is time to step aside.

Fall has come, the new semester has begun. I hear the sound of the bell announcing the beginning of classes, and see young freshmen, like confused and distracted ants, make their way to their appointed rooms, peering anxiously at campus maps. I picture my old friend Bob emerge out of his office head bent, shoulders drooping with the weight of books and folders precariously balanced under both arms, and young Mark, teacher of the twenty-first century, books in backpack, laptop slung across his shoulder, stride purposefully across the hall. I don't know what my office looks like now. Lopa, who is its new occupant, will have given it the mark of her own personality, which is just how it should be. The old depart, the young step in, and life goes on, like a river, its water disturbed momentarily by inevitable comings and goings, and then closing over again. I have stepped out of that river and I watch its flow now with a friendly but detached interest.

"I'm fine," I reported to Sat in India later in the day. "I thought it would be wrenching, this end of a life time of teaching. But I feel tranquil and at peace."

"That's because you did it to your heart's content. You can look back without regret and say, 'It was a fruitful and fulfilling life.'" *Docie rework*

"True, but what next?" I asked. "Grow old and wait for death?"

"We're already old," he reminded me. "I looked in the mirror the other morning after I woke up. My hair looked like dried tufts of grass, and my face was all pulled down like a wrinkled glove. I looked like one of those corpses we used to pull out of drawers in the morgue for dissection. The gap in my upper jaw from the tooth I lost last year didn't make it any better."

"I know. I don't look in the mirror much any more. Youth has its own storms and earthquakes, but they come in different forms for each of us. The miseries of old age are the same. Growing old, I must say, is the hardest thing we have to do."

"You don't have to do anything to grow old. You can stand still in one place and do nothing, and you'll still lose your teeth and look dry and withered."

"Like Prince Andrey's battalion at Borodino. Half of them got killed without raising a weapon, as they stood still in ranks waiting for orders to attack."

"Who is Prince Andrey?"

"Tolstoy's *War and Peace*," I said.

This conversation wasn't going in a very cheerful direction. I tried to put a more stoic face on it. "In any case, as Seneca

18

says, if the stones with which we build our houses crumble within our own life time, what can we say about ourselves, who are mere flesh and bone?"

"I can't hear you. Your voice is breaking up. Did you say Seneca? Who is Seneca?"

"Nero's tutor." There was silence at the other end. The line had got disconnected. I sighed, and dialed my sister Bui. "Today is the first day of my retirement," I told her.

"It is?" she replied, distractedly. "I had a terrible dream last night. It was Yama (the god of death). He was dressed in black and he stretched out his arm to me in silence. I reached for my Gita but I couldn't find it."

"'Death is near, and black, not at a distance/not to be evaded,'" I thought aloud.

"What did you say?" she asked, puzzled.

"Oh, nothing. It was Homer."

"Who is Homer?"

"Never mind. What were you saying?"

"I was telling you about my dream." Bui continued, "Hai! It was horrible! I couldn't go back to sleep, and the next day all day, I looked at pictures of poor Deshian. Our sister Sudesh died of cancer four years ago. I was by her side the day she died. I remember every moment of that day. Her face had turned all black. It was as if the blood in her veins had turned to water, but there was red blood coming out of the side of her mouth. I held her hand and kept calling: 'Deshian, I'm here! Can you hear me?' But she was lost to this world. Her soul tried to leave her body, but it was trapped like a little bird in a cage. Hai! I'll never forget the moment when they put her body in the crematorium, and the door closed. 'Deshi, are you really gone?' I said in my heart. I felt as if my own soul had left my body."

We've had this conversation a hundred times these four years. I listen, she talks. The same grief, the same memories, the same lament, the same simple, unadorned, facts of hateful death, and the wounds it leaves in the hearts of those who witness its ravages. I tell Bui again the dream I had one day shortly after Sudesh's death: I call the operator and ask her to connect me to Delhi. "The line is busy," she says. "Please hold while I try again." As I hold, I hear voices, some close, others distant, but I can't make out the words. Just as I put down the phone, I realize one of those voices had been Sudesh's. I redial frantically and I hear her

19

voice again. "Is that you, Sudesh? Deshi, is that you?" I shout over the other voices. "Don't go! Speak to me!" And I woke up, crying.

"Are you crying?" Bui asked.

"Yes, thank you," I said, through my tears. "Now I'll stay awake all night."

"Don't cry. It was fate. Who can turn its hand? What was destined to happen will happen. When your time comes, no medicine can save you, not even God. That is the harsh reality. We have to adjust."

"True. Homer would have agreed."

"Again Homer! Forget Homer. Try to sleep. You have to go to work in the morning. It's morning here and I have to clean the house and go to the market to do some shopping for lunch. I don't feel like eating, but I have some guests coming this after-noon. Good night."

"I told you I retired today. I don't have to go to work, silly."

"Oh, I'm sorry, I forgot! Don't hang up. I don't have to go to the market. I just made up that story to let you go to sleep. Were you hurt? Let's talk. You retired today. What can I say? I will never have to face that day, because I never had a job. I am just a simple person. I don't have a college degree, like you. You'll have to adjust. Having a routine helps. Keep yourself busy. That's what I do. When are you coming? You can come any time you want now; you are free as a bird!" And we talked late into the night, just as we do when I visit her and Savita, our youngest sister, every winter in Delhi, and made plans for my coming trip next year to go see the peacocks dance in the Rose Garden by her house, and the flowers in Mughal Garden.

My first day of retirement: I had gone from calm detach-ment to rueful laughter to tears of loss and, finally, the sweet solace of love. I had not stepped out of the river, after all. It had just turned another bend, and I will have to navigate this last stretch of its course as I have the bends that I have seen before. It won't be easy, I know. Whoever came up with that saccharine phrase, "the golden years"? Retirement will be no different from the rest of life's "rugged march": "At one place you will part from a companion, at another bury one, and be afraid of one at another" (Seneca, 197).

It has been a long journey, from the foot hills of the Hima-layas where my children were born, to the plains of Delhi; from

20

there, to Ohio, and finally, to what has been my home in Wisconsin since 1988. I have been afraid before of what lay around the next bend, but my life has never been ruled by fear. I've never had any enthusiasm for challenges. My natural inclination is to stay where I am, and enjoy in quiet peace and obscurity my modest pleasures of reading, gardening, listening to music, and seeing the face of a friend at the door. But I've faced the call to action when I had to, and have fought my campaigns, with some honor, when I could neither run nor avoid the arrow aimed at the chest. Not unaided, though. What has sustained me through the years, consciously and unconsciously, is the legacy I inherited from my parents and the world to which they belonged, from which I moved away to find my own world, but to which I return again, in memory, to honor them and what they gave me. In the distance, I can see the ocean, where the journey will end. A look backward, in remembrance and gratitude. Then, onward to the sea!

A Purpose. A Purpose? Enjoy!

"Mm," was all he said. The martini was cold and good. The birch logs crackled in the fireplace. And the little warm garlicky bites were as wonderful as he remembered them. They were the specialty of this, their favorite little hotel in Gstaad.

"And the skiing this afternoon? Did I miss anything?"

She was a good skier and it had puzzled him that she wanted to miss this perfect day on the mountain. For shopping, she had said. That was especially puzzling. She was not a shopper. He liked her indifference to the usual feminine preoccupations. About noon, as he skied into the little village of Rigi and stopped for a glass of wine and a *weisswurst* at the *stube*, it had struck him that she was up to something. It was his birthday. And he was right. It turned out to be a little birthday party for him. She had supervised the hotel staff as they set a table before their fireplace and loaded it with covered platters of the hotel's incomparable food.

"Well, yes you missed a great twenty mile run in perfect snow. And I missed you."

And in fact she *had* gone shopping, and was wearing the fruit of the expedition now. She noticed his appreciative gaze and did a little pose. "You like? It's your birthday present."

A gray silk negligee that clung here and there in remarkable ways. "I like."

It was his seventy-third birthday, and she only twenty-seven, a former student of his who had turned out to be not just the standard English professor groupie, but a real gerontophiliac, excited by his gray chest hair. She liked to kiss his wattled neck. He took the pills that began with the letter that slyly suggested spread legs. Better living through chemistry, as Jerry Garcia used to say. Better living, indeed. She came to him now and sat on the arm of his chair, leaning close. "I hope you didn't feel neglected."

"If I did, the feeling has passed."

There is no doubt that retirement has the potential of turning out really well, particularly if money is unlimited and if one's partner has modeled herself after the heroines of Ernest Hemingway. In my own case, alas, neither condition obtains. As far as I have been able to determine, twenty-something gerontophiliacs exist only in Walter Mitty Land. It's a fine place, WM Land—I visit often—but sadly insubstantial.

When I retired from my English teaching job at a small university in northern Wisconsin, the chancellor gave me a pen and my colleagues in the English Department gave me a blanket. It was a blanket with the university clock tower embroidered on it, a memento of the bastion of learning I had spent a couple of decades at, guiding, herding, in some cases dragging, its student body toward conversance with the higher realms. Or, on some days, putting in my time so I could collect a paycheck. And so they gave me a pen and a blanket—writing and sleeping paraphernalia. And my wife gave me a bottle of good wine. This begins to suggest an agenda, thought I. The thing is to create a satisfying mix. It is a new consideration. During the years of job bondage, the mix created itself. You've got a stack of papers to grade, so do it. Not satisfying? Tough. It's your job, so do it. Now it's suddenly a problem to be worked out. Create a recipe that you find satisfying. It's a sort of IQ test, as in:

Select the pair of words that are related to each other in the same way as the example.

> Example: Employment/Life.
> a. Jail/Freedom.
> b. Marriage/Bachelorhood.
> c. Pole/Pole beans.
> d. Drawstring/Pajamas.
> e. All of the above.

The correct answer is e, of course. The job restricts movement, as jails do, another way of saying that it provides direction. Retiring is a divorce. Tristram Shandy's father said that it is a luxury to sleep diagonally in one's bed. Wives and jobs enforce rectilinearity. Get rid of them and you can sprawl, sleep wherever and whenever. But sprawl feels like freedom only for a time. Then ensues the gormless, formless sensation. One's metaphorical pajama bottoms fall metaphorically off. Wherever and whatever and whenever ultimately need corralling.

A purpose. A purpose? What's the purpose of a purpose? Engrossment. It prevents a life of fluthery flopping about. Purpose can be difficult. Often it is bent out of shape or denied by circumstances. See *Hamlet*. For another example, my friend Fred died a couple of months ago. He had been a photographer. One who made no money at his trade, but he was very good at it. There are lots of talented people in the arts who make no money at it. He was especially fond of photographing nudes. He published a book of excellent nude photographs. Unfortunately, the photographs were accompanied by some very bad poetry. The poetry was written by a professor who taught death and dying classes and they were all about that. The photographs were about anything but that. They were about light and form and beautiful women and were full of life. The two did not go together at all well. It made for a strange book. It was the poet/professor who had access to the publisher and without her Fred's photographs would not have been published. Purpose bent out of shape.

Fred also made a film that won first prize in the Chicago Film Festival. He was on his way. He had purpose, engrossment. Then he got brain cancer and spent twelve years getting chemo and radiation and was sick most of the time. He couldn't work. The photography stopped. He had good days when he felt like working again. The chemo had been effective and he was up and around. We, with wives and friends, went out to dinner a few times. Then one day he went upstairs to take a nap and died in his sleep. The treatments had been too much for his heart. Purpose denied.

The gift of life, as the preachers call it, is sometimes a Christmas necktie, a bright blue one with yellow pineapple slices on it. Who or whatever put the whole idea of the gift of life together seems not to have thought out the shape of it well. Lots of vim and hilarity accompanied by bone-headed know-nothingness is the condition known as youth. It gradually morphs into sleepy moping out-of-itness, then an illness of some random length selected by some god of misery. Then exit, shuffling ever more slowly. No music. No grand finale.

And other friends have died. My friend Betty. Former professional dancer. Pretty. Alcoholic husband, religious proscription on divorce, long wait, love at eighty, death by cancer at eighty-two. Purpose often has not much to do with what happens.

And so do the dramatis personae of one's life diminish in the last act, as they do in tragedies. And we grow weak and silly as in comedies. Oh, she's lovely. I wonder . . . Forget it. To her you're a hundred years old. And I pause with every tinge of pain near any vital area. Is this it? No? OK, then, on I go.

What are the conventions of the last act? One has pretty well sized up the characters, oneself included. Oneself: a concatenation of confusions, buffeted by not-very-hard blows of fate—big pillows of fate, and absentmindedness about one's life, and laziness, the whole mess nearly redeemed at times by the odd epiphany. The measure has been taken. Some real achievement but no world record in anything. Not much chance for one now, or as Jack Teagarden says in his and Louis Armstrong's "Old Rockin' Chair," in response to Louis' "Ain't goin' no where," "Ah done been where I'se gwine."

Character creates the story. So the possible turns the plot can take are limited now. The murders have been committed, the hero compromised. That stab into the arras, bad mistake. Dividing the kingdom, unfortunate. How could I have believed Iago about my wonderful wife? So this is where all those wrong turns and missed opportunities led. Still, it's not that bad. I must have done a few things right. True, there is only one possible ending; even the smart chaps who got a lot farther will have to do the slow shuffle exit.

> There was an old deacon named Clyde
> Who fell through in the outhouse and died.
> A reverent old sexton
> Fell in right next t'im
> And now they're in turd side by side.

So I began with heaven and seem now to have come to hell, the eighth circle thereof if I remember Dante correctly. That's the one where the lost souls become excrement, repeatedly pooped out of sphincters. Most of the time I live between these extremes. Let this

25

now become a Better Homes and Gardens-like guide to happy, or at least tolerable retirement.

Other Things to Do

There are the usual old fart things: play golf, take naps, sit on park benches, write letters to the editor. I've done all of these. Well, not much of the park bench thing—unless it's in Central Park in New York, park bench sitting is too boring for words. And golf is probably a bad habit. I met an old classmate at my fiftieth high school reunion who said he didn't play golf because he hated himself enough already. Naps are a bad habit, too. Afternoon sleepiness and boredom are really the same thing. Get excited about something and skip the nap. That's where the letters to the editor come in.

An example. Our National Guard unit got marched off to Iraq, and, as often happens in war, an entrepreneur saw a chance to make money by it. I wrote a letter to the editor.

To the Editor:

Driving along the residential road that leads to my house a while back, I saw that someone had put an American flag at every corner. They were small flags, about two feet high, and at the base of each was a piece of paper. So, being a curious sort of person, I stopped and took one of the little post-card size papers and had a look at it.

"Support Our Troops," it read in blurry red letters. Below it, in blue, were the details of the departure of Company A, 1st Battalion, 128th Infantry of the Wisconsin Army National Guard, presumably to Iraq. The note requests that we come to the university clock tower at 7:00 a.m. and "bring signs, banners or flags as a way to show our appreciation and to say 'thank you for your service to our country.'"

On the reverse side, under the words "compliments of" is stapled the business card of a real estate agent named Heloise (I have changed her name to protect the guilty) and the words "How can I help you?"

Obviously, this deserved critical comment. So, I commented:

26

This is an open letter to Heloise to tell her how she can help me.

Dear Heloise:

Thanks for your offer of help. We need a lot of help just now. Here's a list of some things that would be helpful.

First of all, Heloise, I would find it helpful if you would not use the American flag to advertise your business. The flag means something serious to many of us, and using it for private profit is inappropriate. (Perkins Restaurants please note.)

Second, it would help if you would stop trying to make a buck out of the war. I know that Halliburton and lots of other big companies are making billions on Iraq, so it must seem harsh that I would complain about you trying to get a commission or two out of it. If I could talk to Halliburton about it, I would. The thing is, people get suspicious about your motives when you do something like that. Do you care more about the troops or about getting listings? As mentioned, you are not the only one with this problem.

Third, it would help our troops if you would be specific about what you mean by the word "support." The Bush administration has cut VA funding, tried to cut combat pay, made troops home from Iraq on leave pay their own air fares, even tried to cut combat death payments— all this to finance tax cuts for his rich supporters. Yet most of the "support our troops" people seem to really mean "be in favor of the war." Make it clear, Heloise, if you would, that the main person who needs to hear the words "support our troops" is George W. Bush.

Fourth, waving flags and banners as our troops go off to this pointless war is probably a bad idea. I wish them well. I hope they all come home safely. But I worry that flag-waving on the occasion of their departure would be interpreted as supporting, not the troops, but this completely misguided war and its incompetent instigators in Washington. I would find it helpful, Heloise, if you would organize a solemn sendoff that would impress on the people who, as they see the families of the soldiers in tears, understand what a sad mess Bush and his administration have gotten us into.

This is my answer to your question. I'm glad you want to help.

Sincerely,

Bill O'Neill

The literary articles I've published elicited almost no response. This non-literary one got quite a bit. Irate letters to the editor, comments from people on the street (all agreeing with me), even a personal letter from a reader in St. Paul, Minnesota saying that she loved my little article. I wrote more political squibs and some of them got published. It was enjoyable, it was purpose. But Bush won. Purpose denied. I haven't written any political articles since the election. What's the point? Political involvement seems to me a simulacrum of purpose. There is lots of motion and passion and hope. But it is the hope of the lottery ticket. You are almost guaranteed to accomplish nothing. Sometimes, as in the case of Mr. Nader running for president in 2000, you do more harm than good. But it does give you some shape and purpose. And being disagreeable can be its own reward. So, why not?

Of course the whole enterprise of trying to apply logical argument to American politics is forlorn and delusional. A friend just gave me a piece of paper with this on it:

The Democrats' mistake was in thinking that a disastrous and unnecessary war, enormous deficits, erosion of liberties, corporate takeover of America, environmental destruction, squandering our economic and moral leadership in the world, and systematic Administration lying would be of concern to the electorate. The Republicans correctly saw that the chief concern of the electorate was to keep gay couples from having abortions.

Books have been written on the dorkiness of the American electorate. There seems to be no remedy.

Another benefit of retirement is you no longer have to suck up to anyone. You can finally say exactly what's on your mind. And the more shocking, the more fun it is. For example:

Margaret, Tom W, Dave H.

God is a meaningless term. Defining an agent (I explain in good professorly fashion) solely by his action with no other information, as in (to crib Bertrand Russell's argument):

Who created the universe?
God.
Who is God?
He is the creator of the universe. That is all we know.

Is logically the same as

Who took my last beer from the refrigerator?
Dar.
Who is Dar?
The one who took your last beer. That is all we know.

The universe is a great mystery. The word God does not help us understand that mystery any more than the word Dar explains where my beer went.

I go on about the vast misery this meaningless and utterly unnecessary term has caused in the world. In proof, here's an excerpt from a *New York Times* article of February 2, 2004:

> At least 244 Muslim pilgrims were crushed do death and a similar number were injured Sunday in a stampede during a Devil-stoning ritual at the climax of the annual haji session in Saudi Arabia.
> Panic spread rapidly after some people in the crowd collapsed just as many of the two million white-robed pilgrims, chanting "God is greatest," surged toward the Jamurat Bridge in Mina to throw stones at pillars representing the Devil.
> . . . Many Muslims believe death on the haji is a gift from God, which cleanses them of sin, and on Sunday the pilgrims continued their rituals, largely unfazed by the disaster.

In the land of my ancestors, the Protestants march annually through the Catholic neighborhoods, taunting them about the fact that the Protestants won the big battle a few centuries ago, which enabled them to take the Catholics' land from them. The

29

Catholics who live on the parade route get ready for this event by leaving a couple dozen of eggs on their window sills for a few weeks before the parade, so they get really rotten. Then they throw the rotten eggs at the Prods as they march by. If by some miracle these people could all become atheists and agnostics what an improvement that would be. And the little Catholic boys would avoid all that buggery.

If there were a benevolent God, wouldn't he help the organized religions of the world to become less idiotic?

Idea for a book: a whole encyclopedia of this kind of thing, entitled *Religion Makes You Stupid*. As soon as I finish one or two other projects, I might start on it.

Near absolute freedom of expression is one of the consolations of old age. The fact that nobody listens to jabbering old codgers is a countervailing item.

So, a rule emerges from this experience.

Rule 1: be cantankerous. No hemming and hawing. Say it, whatever it is. I don't know if there is a rule 2. I'll think about it.

There is another benefit of being old: women will hug you. But the fact that, unless they are young ones (rare), you no longer really want them to is a countervailing item. A person just came to take a picture of my wife, something to do with makeup. My wife's skin is going to become smooth and youthful looking in forty-five days because she's using a new kind of makeup. The sales person wanted some "before" pictures. (That's my trouble. I'm living with a before. I want an after. I'll have one soon, I guess.) The person was an attractive young woman, so I hung around and made jokes. I asked her if she was from *Playboy* magazine and told my wife to take her clothes off—jokes like that. She laughed. The batteries in her camera were dead, so I took the ones out of mine for her to use. They worked. She helped me put them back in my camera. She got close. She probably thought I was just a kindly grandfatherly old guy. These are the further consolations of old age. Sometimes there are no countervailing items.

Rule 2: be furtively lecherous. Don't actually bother young women with your letching. The only part of you a woman under forty is interested in is your wallet. But young women may be enjoyed from a distance. Sometimes quite a short distance.

So, that's about it. Be a cantankerous furtive lecher is about the only advice I've got.

And the thing about purpose—don't feel too badly if you can't find one. In a world where William Bennett gets to write *The Book of Virtues,* intelligent purpose is elusive.

Rule 3: Have a drink.

Thank you. I believe I will.

I'm Telling

I'm telling you stories. Trust me.
It's happening very gently.
You may not notice anything.
It happens very gently,
no wonder we didn't rebel.
At full moon, we gaze upward
and blink. The sun rises
the next day. A hot air balloon crosses
the cloudless sky. It could be
morning or afternoon in whatever
month you choose, whatever year.
And we are old.
It happened very gently.

Night Swim

from *Red Cross Dog*

I go for a night swim
in the dusk hour: so this
is what it's like to live.
I dip, spurt like a dolphin,
heart beating madly
as a muskrat paddles out—
taking the night air
in his city, twirling his moustache.

Evening brings
the slow dark, the panting but
hushed self, elderberry bush
mere shadow. Dog Star,
up there as usual, eyes
us below like so many bones,
protectively. All treachery eased.

Here I am, not in water but,
at this late warm hour, still sitting
on the grassy bank. Maybe it's true,
I can grow old gracefully. Tonight,
I look into the dark with no regret.
I'm happy here, in this body,
these bones, uncomplicated
by glare, heat of sunlight.

Small Lake Up North

from *Red Cross Dog*

It is true, I love this small
round lake—to look at it

is to enter past and future; the lake
was here, the lake will always be here.

I sit, watch it divide itself
into colors. In daylight

it carries my boat, my body. On
calm nights, it holds the moon's reflection

for so long I scarcely notice when,
with the smallest breeze, its silver tray spills—

the lake becomes a plateful of stars.
Tomorrow, when I enter my boat

and row to the center,
I will listen for the loon's call, its

delirium, its undertow of longing—
and know that the lake, hushed under its

surface of nerves, also listens.

Still Center

from *Red Cross Dog*

                    Alone. It's
as if no one else exists anywhere.
And so much noise. The *lip, lip* of
water pressing boat walls; the creak
of oarlock, flick of dragonflies;

lake flat as a table I lay my thoughts
upon, like so many papers: shuffled,
arranged. For the first time
in a long while, no clutter. My mind trim,

in order. I place my hand flat upon water,
feel the stones' weight underneath my boat; feel
fern algae arc and wave; feel the fish, whatever
it is they have for hearts, pumping, ticking.

The shoreline pulls back further.

Writing after Work

Take a rest; a field that has rested gives a bountiful crop.

Ovid

Life with a Cat

I've been out of sorts for months, maybe a year. I don't know why and I don't give a damn. Barb claims I've developed behavior problems common to the newly retired; she thinks I've become a malcontent. "Or, maybe," she conjectured, "something has frightened you." She didn't say what and I was left to wonder what else she thought could scare a man in the second half of his middle years. She's changed too. She used to tell me I was brave, her knight in shining armor. When did that worm turn? Now we sit, two nearly-old people in a corner booth at the China King, nursing cups of tepid egg drop soup and tearing up over hot mustard on a shared spring roll. I watch her slurp tea and squint at me from behind a dragon-faced porcelain cup. "Think of it as male menopause," I tell the cup, "Imagine I've embraced my hopeless and helpless side." She frowned, put the cup down, opened her purse and slid two dollars under the teapot.

"What are you doing?" I asked.

"It's a tip," she said, "and unless you plan to take turns cooking at home, I suggest you leave it there."

"It's a buffet!" I screeched.

So it's true, I've became a malcontent. A malcontent frightened by the very menace I invited, sudden unstructured time. I've taken up daydreaming to fill the void but limit the dreaming to two hours a day, except on weekends when I let it run its unruly course. Daydreaming is strangely addictive even though my brain is addled, the dreams are bad, and I tend to dwell on what one of Barb's self-help books calls ". . . the bristly thread spun from the coarse wool of the repressed memories beast." Is this the sort of thing a thinking person has to write to get published? The guru has a point though. The beast exists, and it can slither in, knock me down and suck the wind right out of my lungs. Oh, I strut defiantly in the face of it of course, but repressed memory beasts are way too strong for a man my age. My resistance is comically unconvincing, even to me. "Breathe, you fake Gulliver," I huff, "be positive." This has over time proven to be a futile plea to the shrinking part of my brain that houses hope. "Weave a complete and balanced tapestry of life from your tangled memory string." More useless self-help garbage. Inevitably, I just let the tapestry unravel, watch it mutate into a disfigured ball, each dangly piece a sordid image remnant.

I have other symptoms; Barb points them out to me. "Now that you're at home more," she says, "I can see what you're up to."

According to her I've become rude to my friends. I offer this explanation, "I see black and white snapshots floating across their eyes, so I stare. Who wouldn't?"

I've been given the gift of anschauung with my engraved gold watch. And my respect for fate is growing. Take fortune cookie messages for example. Fate has chosen me to receive exactly the cookie I finally get. No matter how many cookies are on the table or how agile a shell game I play I can't trick fate into giving me the wrong one. Today's fortune cookie offers this thoughtful advice: "Be careful what you wish for." Then I wonder if caution, like low-fat ice cream, is overrated and may represent an even greater health risk than high cholesterol. Confusing. I fidget when I'm confused and now I read that fidgeting is healthy. Fidgeting burns unwanted calories. Fate.

"Fate, shmate!" Barb says. "You're just rude." She may be right. About a month ago, on a walk to the post office I saw Tom Poreden shuffling toward me. I tried to hide but he caught me. And yes, I was rude.

"You don't look well." he said.

"You've always been a silver-tongued fox," I told him. "Nice to see ya, gotta go." He grabbed my shoulders, did a quick and openly critical survey of my face. He looked concerned, like a fortune teller with bad news.

"Haven't seen you for a few weeks," he said. "Have I missed an appointment?" I asked, using the same caustic tone I lay on telephone solicitors.

He frowned, "You been sick?"

"Don't say that to an old man," I said, "I have years of retirement pay to collect." I poked at his swollen gut, "How's your diet coming?" He shook his head, "You don't look well."

The next morning, sitting on the edge of the bed, I told Barb what Tom said. She swatted at my concern with a flick of her well-manicured fingers. "Ignore him," she said, "you look fine."

"That's what I said," I said.

She was using my shaving mirror to lay down a thin strip of eye liner. I was impressed that she didn't have to blink. "It's just that you're both older now." She paused, lip gloss at the ready. "Tom still wears tie-dye tee shirts for God's sakes," she said. "No one with a comb-over should wear tie-dye." She did a careful finger muss of her just-tinted hair and turned her attention to earrings. "Tom is in denial," she said, "he isn't ready to face the truth."

She tongued the red gloss in a provocative manner, then smacked her lips and chose a pair of silver loops. It's going to be a gypsy-girl day.

"He looks at you and sees himself as an older, not yet old, mind you, but an older man. He can't handle it." She chose a fitted, red top. One of my favorites.

"Thanks," I said. "You've given me something to live for."

"Oh you poor dear," Barb said, "I'm going to have to disappoint you." I got an empathy kiss, then, slippers flopping, she shuffled off to choose a skirt. "There's nothing wrong with getting older, dear," she called out. "What?" I whispered, "I can't hear you when you're in the closet." I tugged at my socks and reviewed yesterday's conversation with Tom. I hadn't told Barb everything. I didn't tell her about the memory fragment.

"Jesus, Tom," I remember saying, "I told you I feel fine." It was annoying that a guy with a Jell-O belly felt comfortable passing judgment on me. How far had I fallen? I looked at a patch of sweat lying in the hollow between his sunken chest and bulging stomach. His shirt was a blaze of lurid orange and yellow around the wet.

"Hey, look at her," Tom jerked his head toward three college girls across the street. His hair lifted, nearly took flight. "I've seen punks before," I said. "Not that one," he said, "the one with the sexy red hair." I saw a snapshot floating in front of his eyes. "Remind you of any one?" He summoned the memory beast.

"Well, maybe," I said, already drifting off, "I guess she looks kind of like a girl we once knew, what was her name . . . Sally something, wasn't it?" I knew her name, of course, it was Powell, Sally Powell. "I guess she looks like that girl Sally something, from the old Clear Lake beer party days," I said. "Sally the prancer dancer."

"Ya baby!"

"Pauly's girl," I said.

"Oh," Tom gushed, "she was wicked wild." He took a deep breath, sucking air through clenched teeth, "And if you ask me, way too much woman for our boy Pauly." His left eye twitched, it might have been a wink.

Barb insists that when I'm with Tom, every person, every thing and every place has its own memory lane address. That's a problem. If she's right I'll never be able to go quietly into the night or wander away from the menacing memory beast. Maybe I need new friends, or I will have to kill Tom so I can start over. That's my fantasy, starting over. But that's all it is, a fantasy. A dead Tom wouldn't fix anything. When somebody dies it isn't like a mulligan for the survivors, it isn't a do-over, or a time warp. Paul Tuccus died and that didn't happen in a parallel universe.

I tried to refocus on Tom's face. A photograph formed where his eyes should be, only a fragment at first, but enough to summon the beast. What emerged was a picture of a beach and a party. Tom, Pauly, and Sally are there, and so am I. We're at Clear Lake, there's a camp fire and a keg of beer. Plastic cups lying in the sand. Heavy smoke from wet wood. We're underage and drunk. I'm skinny and barefoot. I have long hair. Amazing hair. It hangs across my face when I bend over the keg. I'm holding two cups under the spigot. I'm grinning. My front tooth is chipped. One cup is for Sally. She's smiling at me. I look for Pauly. He's missing. Then I see his canoe on the lake, a silver sliver bobbing about thirty feet off shore. I use my imagination, stretch credibility. He's lying down I think, squeezed under the seats.

Maybe. Could be. But why? Probably because he got pissed watching me flirt with Sally. Yes. Or, maybe he's already got himself another prancer dancer girl. Ya. And maybe he's on parade and what he really wants is Sally to see him in his canoe, make her guess what he's up to. But why? Make her jealous of course. Give her a dose of regret. I looked at Sally, she was ignoring the message. There, I think, he has his answer. So it's like

I'm doing him a favor showing him that Sally doesn't care. She's moved on, Pauly! Hell, he should be grateful. "Way to go, Pauly," I yell. "Time to party." I put my hand on Sally's neck, ran my fingers through her heavy hair, whispered in her ear, "Let's go for a walk," I said. And that's when Tom saw Paul's paddle nudging the weeds at the edge of the beach. That should never happen.

Paul loved his paddles, made them himself, his last merit badge project. They were never out of sight and not for loan. Tom howled, "Hey Pauly, my man, you lose something?" His voice bounced heavy over the water. "Shish," I whispered. "Cool it, man." But Tom was a drunk with a powerful secret and he needed to share. "Paul?" Tom giggled, bent over. Hands on knees, he called again, "Paul?" No answer. Tom straightened up, cupped his hands, called like a loon. That was our signal, Pauly's, Tom's and mine, our secret must-contact code. Always answer the loon. But Paul didn't. Surprised and a little annoyed, Tom tried again, "Hey Pauly, you lost your oar, my man?" Silence. I looked at Sally, she was looking at the canoe. She got up, dropped her beer and stumbled toward the lake. It occurred to me that she knew the code and expected Pauly to answer. Maybe she had something she wanted to say to him now, and to me. It was probably a bad sign. She went wading, water up to her waist, tee shirt floating like an orange wreath. She stopped, embraced herself, shivered. Tom yelled, a confused cry this time. Still no answer. Across the lake someone turned a porch light on; a screen door slapped shut.

In the lake Sally started to cry. Drunk, I decided. Damn, she's a morbid drunk. Fantasy interruptus. The water was up to her shoulders. A man yelled "Shut Up" from across the lake. I chugged my beer. Sally swam out to the canoe. It was empty. Someone else found the body.

Accidental drowning the official report read. Alcohol related. The boy fell out of his canoe, the officials guessed, and thanks in part to his over-sized hiking boots, he sank like a rock. At least that's what the cop said that next morning, the big sergeant sitting at our kitchen table.

"All I can charge your son with is underage drinking," he said.

He sounded disappointed. He was a fat man and when his weight shifted his holster squeaked. "But all of this should be part of your permanent record," he said, looking hard at me. "It should be part of his record," he repeated it for my mother's sake. It was early but she was already dressed for church. The cop shifted, squeaked, waited, let the idea sink in. My dad sat, flexed his fingers.

I've found that with unstructured time one bad memory often leads to another. And now I'm haunted by what Tom and I did to a neighborhood boy, a young kid we barely knew.

This is what I remember: A boy from the neighborhood, maybe three years younger than we were, a sixth grader, went deer hunting with his best friend and that friend's new stepfather. It was the boy's first hunt. When they got to the woods, the stepfather, also a new hunter, told the boys to spread out and form a circle. Apparently he thought the idea was to surround the deer. Of course it was a mistake. So the new kid, I don't remember his name, was told to go stand by a tree and be the west-side official spotter. Stay put and keep your eyes open, he was told. There was no chance that would happen. The kid was way too excited and too young to sit still. He had dreams, this boy. His first kill would be a prize buck with a ten-point rack. Naturally with his nerves so frazzled he heard noises he couldn't explain. Maybe animals. Apparently he saw some bushes move in what he thought was an unnatural way, and he shot the noise. Of course it was his friend that he killed.

Awful. A terrible accident and a tragedy. Even then I knew that, but on our way home from school a few days after it happened, Tom and I saw that very kid sitting on the steps of his porch and we yelled "Killer" at him from across the street. "Killer." Staring at Tom now I could hear us yelling "Killer, Killer." This is of course what the guru meant by the coarse wool of the memory beast. When the beast released me I was standing in front of the post office and Tom was talking. He was very excited.

"Hey, my man," he said, "Earth to Carl, earth to Carl, come in Carl." I blinked. "You drifted off there my friend," he said. He was licking his lips, his eyes held the desperate twinkle of a middle-aged voyeur. "Let me guess," he said, "you were picturing yourself with that luscious red haired girl, weren't you. Just the two of you alone on a clothing-optional beach. Am I right? I'm gonna guess you were rubbing warm lotion down her naked back. Am I right?" I shook my head, rubbed my eyes.

"Well, God bless you my creaky friend," he said, "I'm betting imagination is all you got left." He punched my arm.

"I have to go." I said. "I'm feeling sick."

"Told you."

Barb and I have a standing Friday afternoon date. It's a ritual as old as our marriage. It was my week to pick the restaurant. That's not easy now that Barb has become a "no red meat" vegetarian. "For this I got dressed up?" she said when she sat down.

I'm comfortable with institutionalized ritual but unclear about its proper role in my personal life. The pomp and circumstances of a cap-and-gown ceremony at graduation fittingly links the new graduates to their place in the flow of history. But a ritual in everyday life may be just habit and signify nothing more. Is our regular Friday date a bad sign? I don't trust myself to recognize the line between transforming rite and a smothering bad habit. I need a clear, defining "No Trespassing" sign posted where I can see it right there at the badlands boundary. But I trust Barb to know the difference. She's intuitive about these things and I'm beginning to believe in intuition.

We call our Friday ritual the M & M's, a movie and a meal. Now that I'm retired the M and M's have become the center piece of my week.

We sit in the back row of the theater, she channeling Roger Ebert and I Gene Siskel. We finish the review over dinner and a carafe of the house red.

"You're getting worse, you know," Barb said, sneering at the menu, "more secretive." It was a tactical assessment, a calculated prompt meant to prime my chatty pump. "You've always been secretive."

"Have not."

"You worked for thirty years, filled your head with grand ideas and small office politics and you talked incessantly about both. Now you fuss over things that happened over forty years ago."

"I'm going to get the lamb," I said.

"I bumped into Tom a couple days ago."

"Lucky you didn't get hurt."

"He told me you saw someone that reminded you of Clear Lake." She took off her reading glasses. "Is that what's bothering you today?"

She's right of course. I was thinking about Clear Lake. And I hadn't talked with her about it, not lately any way. But to be fair, I did once. I gave Barb the gist of the story when we were dating. Being so young I made it sound like an adventure. Before the wedding she probed for more, "I need to understand who you are," she said. Eventually I showed her the newspaper clippings, Paul's obituary, but I spared her the details, the unreported ugly bits that float occasionally, like debris, to the surface of my mind. I keep those bits to myself, inside where they belong, buried near the center of my inelegant remnant ball, below the surface and out of sight. But Barb is Barb, part playful kitten drawn to a ball of string, and part predator hunter with a latent appetite for red meat. She sat now, quietly dipping something dark and whole grain in a shallow pool of olive oil, waiting for my answer.

"Bump into Tom often, do you?" I asked. "Of course it's probably hard to miss him on your morning run to the gym, especially when he's sitting so conveniently right there in the back booth at The Dew Drop Inn behind a half-empty pitcher of Miller and a basket of salted peanuts." I was going to refer to a couple of greasy, bacon-cheeseburgers just to put her off, but I decided to husband my ammunition. It was a clumsy diversion but it's all I had at the moment.

"You're too young, you know," she said between grainy bites.

"We can tell the waitress you're buying the wine."

This is part of our cat and mouse game. Hide and seek. She's the cat, a patient hunter. I'm the mouse. She's a very good truth mouser. I'm convinced she can smell a secret from the other side of my stone wall. I imagine her waiting for me, licking her paws, grooming herself before eating. "Cats are carnivores, you know," I said a bit too loud. "Of course they are." she said.

The waitress arrived to take our order. "I think I'll have the trout," Barb said. The girl told her it would take about thirty minutes to prepare and Barb said, "That's okay, we have plenty of time." The waitress left. Barb took my hand, "I meant that you are too young to accept a life of guilt." I noticed that she was wearing her anniversary ring. I forgot which anniversary. I filled our glasses. "Here's mud in your eye," I said.

I managed to avoid Tom for a few weeks which helped keep the memory beast at bay but luck failed me outside the post office, again. Tom saw me first. He looked pleased while I wondered if the postal service had started handing out overdue bills to people on the streets. It occurred to me that in the future I should use the drive through. There was no escape.

"Hey, how ya doing, big guy?" he said. "I haven't seen you for what, three weeks? Are ya feeling better?" He stuck his fist out and for an awkward minute waited for the appropriate street smart response.

I was still new to the streets and didn't know how to respond. It finally occurred to him that I wasn't hip to the latest fist-against-fist knuckle-bump greeting, so he punched my shoulder as an act of kindness.

"Another hot one ain't it?" He pulled at his shirt, "Look at me," he said. "I'm sweating like a pig here." The tie-dye lit up like a batik solar flair. "Got time for a cold one?" he said.

It may not have been the same sunburst shirt Tom wore the last time I saw him, but the colors were just as violent and they conjured up the same dark memories.

Pauly made tie-dye shirts. He wore them every day, like a uniform.

Strange. Paul was shy, the kind of gentle spirit that walks unnoticed with hands in pockets and head hanging. I teased him about that, told him that the shirts made him look passive aggressive. Mr. Sneaky Aggressive. The picture faded. I blinked, made the trip back to the sidewalk. This was getting out of hand. Tom was staring at me. What had he asked me?

"I'm not thirsty," I said. I poked at his belly and moved away.

The next M and M Friday was Barb's choice, a restaurant with linen napkins. "So?" she said, after the wine had arrived.

"So what?" I wondered. She took a thoughtful sip, her glass chimed against the flower vase when she set it down. She opened her napkin.

Two droplets of wine, like red sweat, ran down the side of her glass. I followed their voyage until the drops dribbled one by one off the beveled foot, staining the linen. I wondered what that meant. Barb was watching me. "Is today the day?" she said. "Are you going to tell me one of your secrets today?" I was surprised to hear myself say "Yes." The waitress arrived and we ordered. Fish for Barb, salmon, breaded pork chops for me. I kept my menu, declaring an interest in the dessert specials. After a few minutes I glanced at Barb and said, "The rhubarb cobbler looks good." And then, without warning I added, "Sally was sort of Paul's girl friend that summer," as if rhubarb cobbler would remind us both of Clear Lake and friend's drowning. "And I was messing around with her."

I put the menu down. Barb reached for her wine and discovered the stain. She wet her napkin and blotted it. It didn't help. "What did you mean," she asked, "when you say 'messing around'?"

I rolled my eyes, a picture of abused patience. "It means that the night Pauly drowned I was messing around with his girl friend, O.K.?" I gestured, wine splattered my shirt.

"I was getting her beer, chatting her up." Barb wet her napkin again and considered my shirt, "Don't worry," I said, "it didn't go that far." I chugged my wine. "But Pauly didn't know that."

She paused, "So?" she asked. "Wasn't that the point of the night? Drinking?"

"It was my fault that he drank too much," I said. Barb was not impressed.

"Put two and two together," I said. "Why do you think Pauly got so drunk that he couldn't swim? That was my doing."

"Not everything is about you, Professor Carl."

"Hell, he was always passive aggressive."

Barb twisted her napkin, dipped the coiled end into her water again then dropped it unused onto the table. She pushed her chair back.

I wondered if she was going to leave. I waited. She mussed her hair and said, "Did you know that Tom took Sally out a few times?"

"What?'

"He probably knows Sally better than you do, if you know what I mean."

"I don't believe that."

"In his book, Dr. Stuvick says that when people reach a certain age they, retired men mostly, try to rewrite their own history. In their late-middle years men often suffer an orgy of guilt and self loathing. It's a struggle between what has been long repressed and what is an emerging desire to clear one's life slate. Standing at the door of old age they seek forgiveness."

"Forgive me but I think I'll skip dessert." I said.

"Are you feeling remorse or just self pity?" Barb asked.

I sucked my teeth. Our meals arrived, they gave me pork roast by mistake. Barb ordered more wine. I cut my meat into mousey pieces but didn't eat. The waitress came back to ask if everything was O.K. We assured her everything was fine, just fine. We smiled and thanked her. When she left I glared at Barb.

"It was my fault."

"I think you need to do more volunteer work at the hospital."

"It was my fault," I insisted.

"God, you're impossible. If it rains on a million people, it probably isn't because you washed your car. And if your friend drinks too much and drowns it probably isn't because you had the hots for his girl friend. It was an accident."

I drained more wine and Barb fussed with her hair. She looked at my plate. "You need to eat your greens."

"Well, you should have worn your gypsy outfit."

She rubbed her foot against my ankle and said, "Did I ever tell you about what happened to my elementary school friend Debra?"

"No. You need more protein. I'll trade you a bite of pork roast for some salmon."

James Eggert

To Dance in Forbidden Fields

Retirement should be a tasty dessert following a hearty meal. Better yet, a choice of desserts.

Travel. Of course. More time for Mozart and Mahler? Yes. Learning to draw sounds delicious to me. T'ai chi? (I've already started). Plus extra time with friends and family. Or, like my heroes, Henry Thoreau and John Muir, leisure for that unhurried walk in the woods, or an afternoon hiking up Arizona's Red Rocks, or down into the valley of the Redwoods, or simply ambling through a nearby prairie in late summer:

> *So we saunter toward the Holy Land; til one day the sun shall shine more brightly than ever he has done, shall perchance shine into our minds and hearts, and light up our whole lives with a great awakening of light, so warm and serene and golden as on a bank side in autumn.*
>
> *(Henry Thoreau, "Walking")*

When British economist E.F. Schumacher retired from England's National Coal Board in the early 1970's, he felt free to let his mind leap over fences, to "dance" in forbidden fields. Surely some readers recall Schumacher's wonderful book, Small Is Beautiful: Economics as if People Mattered.

In retirement, I too wanted to set aside professional restrictions and write essays that would bridge my lifetime interest in economics with the fields of ecology and spirituality. Here is one example from Wonder of the Tao: A Meditation on Spirituality and Ecological Balance. *It's called:*

49

What's Wrong with Capitalism—A Prairie's Perspective

Despite its materialistic virtues, *something's* amiss in the Land of Capitalism. It's a quality–or *force*–that all too often violates the natural laws that normally insure life's beauty and balance, its health and long-term continuity. To search for that undermining force, let us pretend for a moment that you could literally pick up Market Capitalism as if it were a flawed gemstone. Now place it in the palm of your hand and, turning it over and over, inspect it for defects, fissures, and possible flaws. Briefly, what would be the economist's perspective? Now angle it slightly differently: what would be the viewpoint of an ecologist? And finally, is it possible to look at our economy from a prairie's perspective, or that of an old growth forest?

. . .

Economist's Perspective

Economists *do* acknowledge capitalism's imperfections, often describing its defects as "market failures." These include the main unintended impacts ballooning beyond regular business costs into what economists call "externalities," where consumption and profit-making have spill-over effects that all too often damage human health and landscapes, degrade water and air quality, endanger plant and animal species, and possibly, over time, even alter the very stability of Earth's climate. And the remedy?

Corrective measures will usually require government intervention: first to scientifically verify damages, then to initiate policies–such as a "health tax" (on cigarettes), or a "green tax" (on emissions), or the trading of pollution credits, and to enforce clean air, water and endangered species laws, or to negotiate global agreements (e.g., whaling, chlorofluorocarbons, CO^2, etc.) enforced by protocols, regulatory oversight, and international law.

Conceptually, these measures can be understood in the context of motivating businesses and consumers to pay the full direct and indirect costs ("full-cost accounting") of their economic activity, including the costs of collateral damages to natural and human environments. Simply put, it's a fairness issue, of playing the "game" (the "Capitalist Game") fair and square. Let us look at a contemporary illustration regarding human health, a concern that was recently brought to my attention by the Physicians for Social Responsibility, an environmental advocacy group in Washington, D.C.

Childhood Asthma

The issue is the ever-worsening problem of childhood asthma. Indeed, there's good evidence that asthma is exacerbated by truck and automobile pollution, including elevated ground-level ozone in U.S. cities. Consider the following observations reported by a *U.S. News and World Report* article on the subject of transportation gridlock and urban sprawl:

> During the 1996 Olympics, Atlanta officials took dramatic steps to limit car traffic in the city. The measures worked so well that the number of cars in the morning rush hour dropped by 22.5 percent. But there was another benefit: The number of children suffering asthma attacks, a leading cause of childhood illness, dropped dramatically.[1]

Atlanta's inadvertent "experiment" and its intriguing results dovetail with other studies suggesting that ozone increases the incidence of asthmatic attacks (especially for inner-city children).

Armed with this information, I recently approached a state lawmaker asking if he would consider initiating a modest increase in our state's gas tax (say, one ½ cent) earmarked, not for the usual highway construction and maintenance, but to reimburse parents for asthma-related expenses. I told him that "I was upset because I was paying *too little* for my gas," disturbed that I was "not paying my fair share of the spill-over effects of my driving."

I asked why we should force families with sick children to subsidize an artificially low-cost transportation system. Relevant expenses might include:

- emergency trips to the hospital,
- wages lost attending sick children,
- asthma medication, inhalers, charcoal-impregnated face masks,
- doctor's fees and higher insurance premiums.

Drivers, I said, should also be responsible for the extra costs of rescheduling outdoor sporting events, since many asthmatic children are forced to remain indoors during periodic ozone alerts. An increase in our federal and/or state gasoline tax would be a

---

[1] Phillip J. Longman, "American Gridlock," 28 May 2001.

good beginning, a step towards the economist's ideal of full-cost accounting.

Increasing gas taxes would not only help pay legitimate health costs, it would also give a small nudge to many of us to drive slightly less often. In addition, it would motivate some drivers to purchase a more fuel-efficient vehicle the next time they are in the market, including the hybrid cars, and perhaps eventually, fuel-cell cars powered by clean-burning hydrogen.

Ultra small changes in our driving habits—multiplied by millions and millions of drivers—will eventually make a positive difference in air quality. And if drivers were actually paying all of their spill-over costs, they would have a financial incentive to do more walking or perhaps more biking. Studies show that, surprisingly, a quarter of trips are less than one mile, and fourteen percent are less than a half-mile!

Both walkers and bikers in some cities have already pressured government to promote more walkable and bike-friendly neighborhoods. Whereas Atlanta is infamous for its *un*walkabilty, Portland, Oregon, on the other extreme, has some sixteen "Pedestrian Districts" where the street design, sidewalks, and traffic laws give pedestrians priority. And in Davis, California, there are safe, dedicated bike lanes on most city streets. Moreover, developers in Davis are required to provide bike access to new residential and commercial developments.

Full-cost accounting would also encourage more car pooling and, if available, greater use of public transit. Not only would urban adults and children breathe easier, but trees and wildlife would too. And finally, if truckers and car owners paid their full direct and indirect costs, economists believe it would begin to reduce road congestion while diminishing the political pressure to widen roads and highways and thus minimize damage to local communities and to the landscape itself.

Of course the economist's perspective—even with good science, logic, and sensible remedies on its side—is usually no match for well-funded special interests. In the case of increasing gas taxes for legitimate spill-over costs, the powerful highway, oil, and automobile lobbies will often block legislation that would (as they see it), "harm" their industries. Indeed, in response to my gas tax suggestion, my representative told me, "I understand your point and yes, I even agree with you," but then added: "Jim, you'd better forget it; politically it ain't going to happen."

Ecologist's Perspective

I dream of a day when among others, parents, children, politicians, economists, CEOs, bankers, miners, loggers, etc., make decisions based upon a genuine ecological consciousness, including an understanding and full appreciation of the broad spectrum of environmental values that allow ecosystems to be healthy and whole.

As an example, consider an old growth forest, such as the few that still exist in the United States. In what ways would the ecologists' perspective differ from that of a for-profit capitalist? To answer this question, I find it helpful to picture in my mind an image of a playground teeter-totter that has a large, colorful basket at each end. The basket on the left side represents *Capitalist Values* and the one on the right proclaims *Ecological Values*. Next, children at each end begin placing weighted objects representing the two different sets of values. What weights would they put into the capitalist basket? Benefits might include:

- the monetary value of wood products (including export earnings), incomes for loggers, truckers, and sawmill operators;
- increased sales for equipment, including manufacturing jobs;
- an increase in the company's short-term profits;
- corporate stock price that would go up adding value to stockholder portfolios.

Importantly, from the "for-profit" point of view, there would be pressure to maximize these values in the short run by clear-cutting the forest.

Now turning our attention to the right side (ecological values) what representative "weights" would the children put into their basket? Of course, in some old growth forests (such as the Menominee Indian Reservation in Wisconsin), logging provides modest economic benefits plus the tribe has been able to maintain their forest's original ecological make-up for generations. The Menominee remove a relatively small portion of the forest each year using a concept of "sustainable yield management principles" that incorporates selective cutting based on cultural constraints laid down by tribal elders over a hundred years ago. With selective cutting strategy, there would be some monetary value in lumber, logging, and sawmill operator's jobs, and some export profits. But

53

the return in the short-run would be lower (compared to clear-cutting), yet over many years, income would be relatively stable.

Now in addition to the modest economic benefits, let's ask the children to put into their basket the following "weights" representing a broader spectrum of ecological, scientific, and spiritual values:

- a habitat for endangered plants and animals;
- the possibility of discovering new and effective wonder drugs from the forest's plant life;
- a "living classroom" to study a healthy ecosystem;
- a source of beauty, inspiration, and spiritual sustenance;
- cooler, cleaner, and healthier streams and rivers (compared to a clear-cut forest);
- the recycling of nutrients and the production of new topsoil;
- the ability to sequester atmospheric carbon and generate oxygen.

Tropical forests may also produce a sustainable supply of nuts, berries, valuable barks, tubers, mushrooms, and medicines for those who know how to find them. From an ecological perspective, forests roll up their sleeves, so to speak, and work hard to provide invisible, yet important benefits or so-called ecological services based on the productivity of the forests' intrinsic natural capital.

In comparison, the children's ecological-values basket ought to easily outweigh the capitalist basket. Yet in our current global economic arrangement of ultra-powerful forces of corrupt politics, obsession with unfettered free trade–plus, of course, inflated greed and short-run profit maximization, we find that the capitalist basket usually wins out. It's as if the global economy were (metaphorically) defying gravity as well as other vital laws of nature.

The Prairie's Perspective

If I were asked to pick an analogy from which I might learn the principles for a future capitalism, some would think my example to be a little odd: my choice would be a native prairie ecosystem I walk through nearly every day. It's not exactly *global* free-market capitalism, but more a living example of what might be called *local* natural capitalism. Indeed, my prairie has become a mentor for me—as if it were trying to teach its lessons to a slow-learning, yet earnest economics student. Nevertheless, I have now discovered that this flowering grassland is not only attractive, but exceptionally diverse, and, like a model sustainable economy, remarkably productive—turning sunbeams into biotic beauty and eventually converting vegetation into rich, deep, loamy soils.

In addition, this prairie ecosystem has achieved something quite amazing: an exquisite balance between life and death— humming along year after year in a kind of steady-state, economic efficiency. It recycles virtually everything and unfailingly, it blooms anew—spring after spring and every summer too!

Prairies are resilient in severe drought; yet they can also handle a week of drenching rain. Moles, monarch butterflies, and meadowlarks survive there. Blue stems and Indian grasses live in prairies too, and so do black-eyed Susans, purple prairie clovers, stiff goldenrods, and late-summer blooms of blazing stars.

Time for sauntering through the prairie? Yes.

But sometimes I also enjoy simply lying down, accepting gravity as it were, my back stretched out along the rough ground, my eyes taking in sun, cloud, flower, seedpod, and there high above me, tufts of grasses bending down and up, up and down, as if there were an invisible ocean of windblown waves. With eyes half-closed, I daydream of dancing with a butterfly who flits and flutters between the flowers.

So one might ask: "What direction, what trajectory will we be able to follow to a more natural, indeed a more *balanced* capitalism?" Can our economy readjust and redress its spill-over effects and correct its corrosive externalities? Can we conserve (as if an ecological consciousness were our second nature) our planet's grasslands, soils, ancient forests, subterranean waters, its oceans, rivers, and reefs? Like the prairie, can we find a more harmonic, natural equilibrium that abounds in beauty, balance, and biodiversity? And finally, can we utilize renewable energies and make consumables durable (and fully recyclable) while preserving Earth's realms of amazement, its landscapes of surprise?

The Write Stuff

When, at the age of sixty-two, I made a deal with the university where I was teaching that I would retire when I was sixty-five, I had plenty of time to think over my alternatives. At first, I wasn't worried about such dreadful possibilities as
- Having too much time on my hands,
- Running out of money before I was sixty-six,
- Driving my wife, Judy, crazy by hanging around the house all day, or
- Running out of books to read.

Judy and I planned to travel as extensively as our budget would allow, and, when at home, I had projects I looked forward to completing. For example, when I left the university I intended to begin research that might lead to the publication of a book. That project alone would probably consume two or three years, and I envisioned the possibility of writing other books when that one was completed.

But my complacency began to erode as time went on.

A faculty member who occupied the office next to mine was scheduled to retire at the same time as I was. He had been teaching at the university for more than forty-five years—it was the only full-time job he ever held—and, for him, retirement was a crisis to be dreaded, not an opportunity. Virtually every morning, he would say to me with a hangdog expression, "What am I going to do if I don't have a ten o'clock class to teach? Why should I get up in the morning? *Will* I get up in the morning?" After hearing a variation of those agonized questions virtually every day for more than two years, I began to worry. Maybe this retirement thing won't be as easy as I'd thought.

Adding to my growing sense of dread was the more-than-occasional bug that Judy put in my ear during dinner on most evenings. "You've got to have a plan," she said earnestly, "a *concrete* plan, a day-to-day plan. It's not enough just to say that you're going to write. The question is, what will you do on Tuesday?"

"Maybe I've been too casual about retirement," I thought. So I began buying books about meaningful retirement pursuits and making lists of all the things I might do to occupy my time. I could volunteer to deliver hot meals to shut-ins; I could take a more active role at my synagogue; I could plan to read three books every week; I could take up golf; I could send e-mails to all the friends I hadn't been in touch with for years; I could have lunch every day with my faculty colleagues at the university cafeteria; I could open a small business (although what sort of business it might be and what I was qualified to do was a mystery to me).

But I was prevented from making a detailed plan for several reasons. For one thing, I had several retired friends who, whenever I asked how they were doing, said, "Where does the time go? I used to think I was busy, but it's *nothing* compared to all the activities I'm involved in now." I know that that reply should have put my fears to rest, but it had the opposite effect. I wasn't the sort of person who wanted to retire in order to become busier than I had been. For several years I'd thought how nice it would be to slow down, to do what I wanted to do rather than what I had to do. Was I now going to speed up instead? And if I did, how many years would that take off my life? Additionally, all of the activities I had been contemplating (i.e., play golf, open a business) failed to add up to what I believed to be a satisfactory retirement. And I found that the more I thought about it, the more knots formed in my stomach.

No, I thought, meticulous planning simply won't work for me. I need a goal, that's certain, but beyond that I'd prefer to deal with matters as they arise. The benefit of making this decision was that the knots in my stomach began to become untied; the difficulty, of course, was that I could be wrong. Retirement might be a boring ordeal.

Jump, now, to the present. It's five years since I retired and I'm not bored in the least. I have completed two biographies I was working on (about Alan J. Pakula, the director of *All the President's Men*, *Sophie's Choice*, *Presumed Innocent*, *Klute*, etc., and about Moss Hart, the American playwright who co-wrote such comic masterpieces as *Once In a Lifetime, You Can't Take It With You* and *The Man Who Came to Dinner*, and who directed the original Broadway productions of *My Fair Lady and Camelot*); they were published in September, 2005 and June, 2006, respectively. And I've done some revisions for a new edition of an older book as well: *The Fabulous Lunts,* about Alfred Lunt and Lynn Fontanne, great American stage actors from the early twentieth century through the 1950s. (My other biography, published in 1989, is about Zero Mostel—the original Tevye in *Fiddler on the Roof*—and one of the victims of blacklisting in movies and television). I seem to have developed a specialty—theatrical biographies—although I never made a decision to do so. It's just that after writing my first biography, I learned several useful techniques (about interviewing relatives, friends and co-workers of the subjects, about organizing the material to good effect, and about what material should be included and what would be best omitted), and it seemed wasteful not to apply those to another. Then, having refined those techniques, it led to a third such book, then a fourth.

One of the joys of writing biographies has been the interviews, for I have spoken to many fascinating and articulate people. I have always believed that most theatre people are particularly intelligent, analytical, and congenial, and my interviews have confirmed that again and again. At the risk of seeming like an insufferable name-dropper, I would count the following people among the most knowledgeable, cooperative and helpful I've interviewed: some of them, like Uta Hagen, Alan Hewitt, Kitty Carlisle Hart and John Randolph, are no longer alive; but Sheldon Harnick, Larry Gelbart, Julie Andrews, Kevin Kline, Meryl Streep and Robert Redford are still around and are all highly productive.

I have also written seven plays since retiring. I've made no effort to publish any of them because, for me, the desired result of writing a play is to see the play in production—and, happily, all but the play I've just completed have been produced. Many of them I've directed myself. My professional responsibilities at the university included directing plays, which I did on a regular basis. As a result, I developed a love for directing long ago, which is at least equal to the satisfaction I receive from writing.

Recently I've become involved with a new and vital theatre group which has given me an opportunity to write for a specific space and group of performers, to direct, and, on one occasion, to resume a long-dormant acting career. One of the things I always found most appealing about working in the theatre before I retired was the communal effort involved in putting together the best possible production. I still feel that way, and still take great satisfaction when a production turns out to be all I hoped it would. An incidental benefit is that the friendships one makes when involved in a theatrical venture are intense. They may dissipate after the production has ended its run, but during the rehearsals and performances, actors, directors, designers and stage managers bond in the most remarkable way.

And—as Judy and I had hoped—we've traveled regularly, both inside and outside the U.S. We've been to Alaska, upstate New York (where we both attended college), California (often; it's where our two children and their spouses live), New Orleans (before Katrina), Florida (for a week during spring training), New York City, Spain, Sicily, Italy, China, Argentina, Brazil, Chile, Norway, Sweden, Finland, Thailand, Hong Kong, Singapore . . . Just typing the list is enough to bring on the memory of long airline flights and weeks of jet leg. Planning the trips alone has taken up nearly as much time as the trips themselves, adding to the sense of fatigue which sometimes overcomes me. I have to be careful, I keep reminding myself. I don't want to travel just because it will keep me busy; I want to travel because it's an exciting adventure. If any trip *doesn't* hold the promise of excitement, I should stay home and work on the book or play I'm engaged on.

Not that we're finished traveling, mind you. Next year we're thinking about taking a trip to Japan and we'd like to return to France in the not-too-distant future. As much as I may complain about the long flights, the jet lag, etc., I've never failed to enjoy any of our trips. And twice in recent years Judy has attended her high school reunion in Virginia; I imagine she'll continue to do so, although, since I know no one from her high school, it would take heaven and earth to get me to accompany her. I can visualize a large group of alumni who have shared a fifty-year history in a cluster, chatting excitedly about the past, while I, together with another spouse or two, drink ourselves into oblivion at the cash bar.

Retirement has had other rewards. I've had time to go to a gym three days a week and tone muscles that were in danger of become atrophied. Every Friday afternoon I attend "The Seminar" (comprised of a group of former academics who meet to drink beer and wine—or, in my case, Bloody Marys), where we all talk about places we've traveled, books we've read, concerts we've attended, plays and movies we've seen. I *have* increased my reading, and I've enjoyed most of the books I've read. I've subscribed to a few magazines I always said I'd like to get, and if I don't always have time to read them, well, I pile them up in the possibly deluded belief that I will find the time someday. And, I am glad to say, I have not driven Judy crazy by my increased presence, although I won't take credit for that; the fact that we work in separate offices in our house, use separate computers and work on separate projects undoubtedly has more to do with her continued sanity than anything else.

On the negative side, I'll admit that I *do* miss teaching. I enjoyed working with university students, and the fact that, when I stop by the departmental office to pick up my mail few of the students recognize me any more, is a bit off-putting. However, I returned to the university to teach one course last semester and I've taken to mentoring a student at the local state university, and both experiences proved to be gratifying ways of maintaining my involvement with idealistic young people of college age. So my only reservation about retirement is not particularly troublesome, after all, for I find that I've gained a good deal more than I've lost as a result of my decision to retire. Of course, I could wake up next Tuesday with nothing to do, and boredom might set in quickly. But I only have to think of a new idea for a book or a play, or arrange to direct a production for Heartland Theatre to get the juices flowing again, so I'm not really worried.

My philosophy about retirement boils down to this: developing a general plan is a good idea, but too much planning can cause knots in your stomach and is—for me, at any rate—a ritual to be avoided. Why try to schedule every moment of your day for the next fifteen years when, if you have a few activities that bring you pleasure (including at least one overriding activity that also brings fulfillment), that's all you really need?

Erik Thurin

*Erik kept notes and journals from 1950 until the end of his life in
2005. During his retirement he wrote two full-length memoirs,
published two scholarly books, and left an unfinished manuscript
on Emily Dickinson. He wrote once that to end one's professional
life abruptly and devote all the time left to leisure activities would
be tantamount to being "already sporting in the Elysian Fields."
His energetic reading included novels and poetry in the original
as a way of keeping up his many languages. He never allowed
anyone to read his journals, preferring to leave them to posterity.
Reading them now is both difficult and wonderful. – ST*

Never Alone

*I am not solitary whilst I read and
write, though nobody is with me.*

Ralph Waldo Emerson, *Nature*

(12 May 1993) The chancellor's reception for retiring faculty . . . A former dean came up and introduced himself, as if I had
never seen him before. The only relation between us, he informed
me, had been through my writing—he had read my books.

(17 May 1993) Waked up by a bird flying into the bedroom window above my head again and again. The bird in
question must think he sees another bird encroaching on his
territory. It must be the mirror stage I have been reading about in
Lacan's *Ecrits*.

(23 May 1993) I have never seen *Cheers*, so I will be unable to miss the show that is now finally off the air.

In the morning I heard Susan suggest that Al Gore has
been reduced to walking around hugging trees. In the afternoon I
came upon a passage in which Lacan quotes Plato's references to a

certain class of philosophers who in their eagerness to commune with nature went around embracing trees.

(8 June 1993) Foucault's *History of Sexuality*: He clouds what is clear and obfuscates the obvious. An extraordinary verbal facility allows him to defamiliarize the familiar. His exposition is often so abstract and scant of evidence that it is hard to judge whether he is right or not. But it would seem that his way of arguing that society has not repressed sex but deployed it during the last few hundred years is largely a play with words. At the most he achieves a slight shift of emphasis.

(12 June 1993) I am finally having some time to spare for the editing of my notebooks.

(20 August 1993) Dinner-party talk about Greece, Bill and Jan having just returned from their Aegean cruise and Ray and Florence are leaving for theirs in a couple of weeks. I realized that my own first-hand experience of Greece (1978, 1956, 1951) is no longer up to date. But I am not letting that bother me. The older one's experience of Greece, the better.

(October 1993) People keep congratulating me on my retirement. I do not mind the hypocrisy as such, but the *need* for hypocrisy has me worried: is retirement, then, the end of everything?

We used to say—Bill still says—that we teach for the few, the exceptional students, who justify the effort. Over the years they are not so few. I just counted the A's (and A-'s) I gave in the 35 sections of Classical and Biblical Literature I have had over more than twenty years: There are 167 of them. The standards may have fluctuated a little (there is a big bulge in the numbers beginning with the fall of '74 and ending with the spring of '76, that is, after I published the *Universal Autobiography*, and another, less drastic one in the spring and fall of 1981 as *Priest of Pan* was being published, but those 167 students cannot have been that bad. If one wants to be more strict one can look at those who got A's on all their essay tests. I used to brag that those who got A's on all of my essay tests would be successful at any university. Well, there were 41 such students in Classical and Biblical alone.

I have to confess that I do not remember those 41 students; they are just names on the rosters. I do not even remember Sarah Bowker (fall of '81), who, judging by available data, may have been the best—certainly one of the very best—of all the students who took my course in Classical and Biblical Literature.

(18 October 1993) Sitting on the couch in the evening re-reading Genesis in the original is still the best part of the day. Got to the *Akedah* today. Remember from the last time Plaut's remark about the staccato nature—suggesting sleep-walking state of mind—of the phrases describing Abraham's taking Isaac to the place where God had told him to sacrifice his son. But I am more able to appreciate this stylistic trait now.

(12 December 1993) Shocked (in a manner of speaking) to find that Barthes plagiarizes Huysmans when he characterizes Mallarmé as a murderer of the French language (with French literature as its carcass). Huysmans makes the same nonsensical point, with infinitely more style, at the end of chapter XIV.

(21 December 1993) Reading the poetry of Ruben Dario: Wait a minute—talent is at work here. All poetry is rhetoric of one kind or another. If Ruben Dario substitutes words for reality, he does so with aid of a language he has forged himself: a traditional-poetic (classicist) vocabulary couched in the latest impressionist syntax. It is rhetoric raised to a higher power, a ritual-sensual language that does not need anything beyond itself to yield satisfaction. The medium is indeed the message in this case. An argument is present, of course, and discernible under the brilliant linguistic surface, but it often seems to play only a supportive role. The language sounded better than it does, draws attention to itself. Spanish has never *sounded* better than it does in pieces like *"Acuarela," "Un retrato de watteau,"* or for that matter *"Palomas blancas y garzas negras."*

Not surprisingly, Hugo is the "god" of this poet. His syntax also suggests an affinity with prose writers like the Goncourts and Huysmans. If I had read him earlier, I would probably have quoted an expression or two in my study of Whitman. Incidentally, one of the final sonnets called *"Medallones"* is "Whitman."

(8 January 1994) I have been re-reading *The Sun Also Rises* in the hope of reconstructing my 1958 reaction to the novel. To get back to it I have to pass through the impression I got teaching it at Stout quite a few years ago. . . . In those early days I appreciated the novel mainly to the extent that it spoke to my *aspiration*. It reflected a life-style—the alleged life of a writer abroad—that seemed infinitely more attractive to me than teaching Latin and Greek in Varberg [Sweden]. The novel looks different today when that aspiration has been fulfilled or rendered obsolete by advancing age.

(4 February 1994) I used to be defined by what I read, had read, or could read. More and more I am coming to be defined by what I write, have written, and can write?

(12 March 1994) I remember telling Bankel [an old friend in Sweden] back in 1965 that I was checking off item after item on a list of things I had to do before leaving for the New World. Is it time to make another check list, of things that ought to be done before my departure for the next world?

(22 May 1994) *Pickwick* gets a bit tedious as the serializing drags out. In the end Dickens himself seems glad to be quit of his characters. I am, however, as fascinated by the vocabulary of some of his characters as I am by Jingle's syntax. Phrases like "hang out" and "a go," which I had always thought of as modern American slang, are already used in their present sense.

(26 September 1994) Reading *Walden* in the evening. Sometimes I feel as if I had never really done that before. It is one thing to prepare to teach a book, another to actually read it. Take "Higher Laws." I remembered it as a chapter in which Thoreau goes out on a transcendentalist limb and in essence rejects human biology; based on my superficial teacher's reading I had dismissed it as unsuitable for a literature class at Stout. But a closer, more scholarly reading shows that there is no one-sided rejection of the human condition. On the contrary, there is a surprisingly well-balanced argument. This is the chapter Thoreau begins by telling us about catching a glimpse of a woodchuck on his way home from the woods and being seized by an impulse to devour him raw, "not that I was hungry then, except for that wildness that he represented." And get this: "I found in myself, and still find, an instinct toward a higher, or, as it is named, spiritual life, as do most men, and another toward a primitive rank and savage one, and I reverence both." Extending this balancing act, Thoreau goes on to argue that while he has given up hunting and is about to give up fishing, he does not imagine it is making him more humane. These activities represent an important phase of human experience, and it is perfectly all right for New England boys to engage in them—as long as they do not get stuck at that stage: truly coming of age means discovering that there is bigger game to hunt and bigger fish to catch. (After that one is more ready to hear that meat-eating is unclean business and that chastity is the flowering of man.)

(20 October 1994) In a way I am surprised that my Whitman study is being published. It may not be quite as "special" as some editors who turned down earlier versions of it thought or pretended to think, but it certainly is the most original book I have written to date. I went out on a limb when I began it.

(22 October 1994) What I liked best in *Death in a Tenured Position* is an epigraph quoting Virginia Woolf: "I sometimes think only autobiography is literature." It reminds me of Henry Miller's quotation from Emerson in the epigraph to *Tropic of Cancer*: "The novels will give way, by and by, to diaries or autobiographies, captivating books . . ." I do not want to do what so many aspiring novelists seem to do: change the first person to third. I will be shamelessly autobiographical.

(10 November 1994) I picked up some brochures about vacations on Tahiti and Hawaii at Sunshine Travel. Tahiti . . . Papeete . . . Bora Bora . . . But such a trip seems rather pricey and the traveling would be grueling. How would a sixty-five-year-old feel on arrival? Right now I feel I have had the best part of the experience by reading about it and looking at the pictures.

(1 February 1995) Unlimited leisure and my word processor should enable me to work at least twice as fast as in the past. Yet I would be a fool to start another scholarly project before I have seen the critical reaction to *Whitman Between Impressionism and Expressionism*. . . . A problem with retirement like mine is that it makes life too easy. One drops one's guard, and when stamina is needed, one may no longer have it.

(6 May 1995) You feel like a criminal exiting and entering your house these days. Susan put a plastic bag over the light fixture to prevent the finches from building a nest on it. They did anyway, and right now the female is sitting on her eggs; she gets very upset when you open the door. On the other side, in the evergreens, a robin is sitting quite openly on four blue eggs.

(25 June 1995) The press sent me a copy of the *Choice* review of *Whitman Between Impressionism and Expressionism*. I am introduced as "a classical philologist and respected American literature scholar." That sounds like recognition at last but suppose it is just an echo of the autobiographical information given on the cover?

(14 August 1995) Played croquet with the grandchildren in the morning. Alex again shows that he is a wit: When I told him

at the breakfast table, "Be calm, be composed," he retorted, "I am not a piece of music."

(21 August 1995) Kristina and Alex write their Christmas lists. Alex fires off a letter to Santa Claus.

(7 September 1995) Finished *Possession*, after skipping some of Ash's and Lamote's writing. Thought for a while I might go back and read the book more carefully one day. But maybe I won't. Byatt has talent, a lot of talent, but in the final analysis the book is not so much an academic novel as an academic Gothic romance (she quotes Hawthorne on the difference between *novel* and *romance.*)

(21 September 1995) A strange thought comes now and then as I work on my autobiographical novel: my analytic and imaginative powers do not seem to have been touched by age. Suppose I am one of those exceptions. Suppose I shall be writing for a long time yet?

(25 September) Have been using *Idiot* as evening reading for some time now, and it is funny how my mind—without any conscious effort on my part—tries to express itself in Russian (sometimes in the middle of the night.)

(31 December 1995) Puerto Vallarta . . . we passed a place where some pushers of time-shares were stationed. As we sauntered by without paying any attention to their siren noises, I heard one of them wondering loudly in excellent English if I was not "a famous professor," answering himself that I was sure to be "something like that." At first I thought he was jeering at me, but on second thought I decided that he was flattering me in the hope that I would stop to hear him out.

(15 January 1996) Sometimes it seems to me that I may be waiting for something other than reviews. What? I hope to God it is not Godot.

(16 January 1996) Theory: It seems ironic, when you have rejected French in favor of English and American literature, to find Anglo-Saxon critics groveling before the likes of Barthes and Derrida, not to mention Lacan, Lyotard, and Foucault.

(1 February 1996) A report on the 5:30 news suggests that "even old people" can grow new brain cells by continuing to challenge themselves intellectually. Physical exercise is supposed to support such new growth by increasing the blood supply to the brain. What about strokes resulting from excessive intellectual effort?

(21 March 1996) I do some exploratory work on my various scholarly projects now and then, but I always end up wondering if it is worth my while doing anything of this kind at this point. One has to know when to stop, leave good enough alone, quit while one is ahead?

(6 May 1996) I love the Finnish language as I encounter it in *Pakolaiset*. It is one of the oldest items in my intellectual baggage, and it was foolish to want to jettison it.

(10 November 1996) One reason why I am writing another scholarly book [*The American Discovery of the Norse*] seems to be that it connects me with something outside myself. It is also, more tangibly than autobiographical writing, life in the process of being lived, I feel less retired.

(25 November 1996) I always feel slightly embarrassed when Jim, my barber, asks me what I am doing with myself, as he regularly does. But the best thing is simply to confess the truth: I read and write.

(24 February 1997) Once more it has been granted me to finish a big project. This one took barely nine months, starting from scratch.

(25 February 1997) Pro/con: In pondering where to move at my age, one must not make the mistake of thinking that one will continue to live forever as one has lived so far. Ought I have a plan for my remaining future? As part of the planning, taking another look at "Imaginary Gender" [about Emily Dickinson] to see if it would be viable as an American literature topic.

(26 February 1997) It is a pleasure to spend the day in one's chair letting one's imagination play on virgin ground.

(4 March 1997) It is not so much a question of making firm plans for your remaining future (how can you do that) as deciding what you *would like* to do with what may remain of your life?

(7 March 1997) Raskolnikov gets to be a bore in the end. . . . Incidentally, the epilogue [of *Crime and Punishment*] stinks.

(16 March 1997) I sometimes wonder if it was a good idea to saddle myself with yet another scholarly scheme. But it has not felt like a burden. It is fun to work on a scholarly manuscript. I am used to doing that. The only problem is that manuscripts are supposed to be published.

(18 May 1997) My yearbooks are neither confessions nor apologia, just records.

(27 May 1997) Once more I am surprised at what I find in my yearbooks. I think recording these things was a kind of unburdening, a way of disposing of them once and for all, making it easier to give my full attention to the rest of my life.

(1 August 1997) I suppose one must make an expensive journey out of Menomonie now and then in order to earn the privilege of sitting at home. One cannot pay too dearly for it.

(2 December 1997) [After first diagnosis of cancer] Creature comforts—small things like afternoon tea, a glass of wine at dinner time—seem to acquire a new significance. Has the universe already shrunk to a tent? One has to fight the feeling that nothing matters anymore. Yielding to it is dying twice.

(31 March 1998) Susan accused me of wanting to die. The thought has occurred to me; there certainly comes a time when you are not only retired but tired, and, I could say, being diagnosed with cancer does not invariably seem like such a big deal if you have pretty much done what you had to do and besides are a sixty-nine year-old male Thurin and likely to die soon anyway (what you chiefly worry about is a futile therapeutic nightmare). On the other hand, I do feel better—and younger—than in November; there are days now in spring when I think I could use a few more years and that my mother's genes would get me them if I could somehow avoid betraying them by dying of cancer or heart trouble inherited from the other side of the family.

(22 May 1999) [At a department party Professor X] kept saying that I looked so good that she thought everyone ought to retire.

(15 April 2000). Bob Dahlke had organized the annual wood-carvers' show at the Thunderbird Mall, and Susan wanted to buy one of his carved birds. There was a kingfisher . . . . I persuaded her to pick that one, sensing it was a literary bird, appropriate for an English department chairman's office. In looking for the literary connection, I discovered that I had confused the kingfisher with the fisher king T.S. Eliot alludes to in "The Wasteland." But then I remembered the poem in which Alcman in his old age tells the choir girls that his legs are failing and that he wishes he were a *kerylos*, a male kingfisher, riding on the back of a *halkyon* or female of the same species. The importance of owning one's own copy of *Lvra Graeca* now became apparent. I could show Susan in black and white that what I was saying was true. She was as pleased with this literary connection as she was to

hear that the kingfisher is the only species of bird in which the female is more colorful and (judging by Alcman's poem) stronger than the male. The connection between the kingfisher and "halcyon days" added to Susan's enthusiasm. As for myself, I kept trying to recite Alcman's poem by heart. It came back to me not wholesale and right off but piecemeal over several hours, like a puzzle in which some pieces would be difficult to find and fit in, when the last piece (*meliqaryes*) slid into its place once I was already in bed.

(14 June 2001) I was tired when my flight arrived at Landvetter [Sweden] where Ann and Jan were waiting for me. But there were no delays because of President Bush. He was to arrive almost three hours after me, and while there were a lot of police around, we had no trouble getting through to Gothenburg.

(1 January 2003) I considered not continuing this journal beyond 2002. It sometimes seems to me that I no longer have any thoughts to speak of and that it might be a good idea to quit by choice at the end of a year just as I began by choice at the beginning of a year. A journal for 2003 might mainly document my mental decline; indeed, I might be forced to quit before the end of the year. In the end, however, I decided that that was a risk worth taking. There might be even fewer thoughts without a journal. Besides, there will be factual events that I can record. One should not deprive old men of their routines.

(3 January 2003) Yes, here we go: my daughter Ann called . . .

(July-August 2003) A meeting of the cousins in Menomonie. Alex and Erik are already fast friends . . . Kristina and Sigrid have hit if off just like Alex and Erik and do not seem to need a larger circle of friends. . . . [The girls] showed unexpected initiative and zeal making meatballs. . . .

"Thank you, Ruth," Erik said to the nametag-wearing woman at the airport check-in counter when she returned his passport. She was overweight, with a dour expression, but she did not resent being treated on a first-name basis by a fifteen-year-old boy. On the contrary, she was visibly charmed. I don't know what she read into Erik's puckish grin, but a thin smile still lingered on her lips as we moved on. . . .

Susan speaks of a "thundering silence" after the grandchildren's departure. But that is an exaggeration. . . . Silence came trickling in, and I easily got used to it.

69

(11 December 2004) It is remarkable how pleasant night can be when one has terminal cancer. Was it the influence of the Christmas tree Susan put up the other day? There were trees in my dream, too, flowering trees exuding balsamic perfume in the darkness of early night. Suddenly I heard somebody calling my name. I did not immediately recognize the voice, but when I did I realized that it belonged to a colleague whom I had had little to do with during my long career. There was, in fact, a congregation of colleagues I had hardly spoken to all these years. Now I felt very close to them, and there was a lot of catching up to do. We played hide and seek among the trees and lit a fire on the shore. Everybody went in the water. I don't remember if we were all naked. I think we were, except for those who were in too exuberant a mood to divest themselves of their outfits before going in. In any case we were having a grand time. My wife can vouch for that. "You had a grand party last night," she said as soon as I opened my eyes. "What did I do?" "You chuckled and swung your arms around as if you thought you were dancing. You spouted a lot of incomprehensible gibberish. You were happy."

Maturing Things

I think age is a high price to pay for maturity.

Tom Stoppard

Beware of the young doctor and the old barber.

Benjamin Franklin

Robert Meier

Eyeing the Retired Building

Since boyhood, I have been a photographer. As a university teacher, I always considered the flexible hours a necessity that allowed me both to have a job that supported my family (teaching English) and to do the work that I love (taking pictures). For me, early retirement from teaching offered the perfect opportunity to dedicate myself full time to photography.

For a long time, my main subject as a photographer has been buildings. In addition to photographing more modern ones, I have had unusual access to old warehouses and industrial structures. These "vintage" buildings fall into two camps that people who have completed a career may well find familiar. Some of the buildings have simply stopped being used in their normal capacity. They are well maintained, in good working order, and ready for a smooth transition to a new use. But other buildings have been entirely abandoned to uncertain fates. Battered by weather, their tenants are rodents and squatters and pigeons. Deterioration and old age have become a part of what they are, haunting and beautiful.

The work depicted on these pages comes from two photo projects I have done that reflect this dissimilarity. The essentially pristine Pillsbury A Mill, built nearly on top of St. Anthony Falls on the Mississippi River in Minneapolis in 1881, was a continuously operating plant until 2003. In the heart of the Minneapolis mill district, it was once the largest flour mill in the world, with water from the Falls directed through the ground floor to two immense water wheels that powered the mill. When I first began photographing the mill's buildings in 2004, about six months after it was closed by its second owner, Archer Daniels Midland, some of the floors in the main building were vacant. Others looked as if workers could readily take up their jobs again. The buildings were heated and fully lighted, machinery was in place, and the only evidence of wildlife was tracks that had been left in the flour dust by mites. The mill was noisy, with the one-man lifts that were used to transport workers through openings in all seven floors, still clanging and banging away.

Of the seven buildings in the Pillsbury A complex, three drew my camera. These were the oldest building of the group, its nearest neighbor, and the far corner building, which contained immense single and double helixes that had been used as slides to transport finished flour. My fascination was with the structural beauty of these helixes. In looking at them, I discovered a key to photographing the Pillsbury A. I had started by using very wide angle lenses in an attempt to capture the vast spaces in the buildings, but I wasn't satisfied with the pictures. For one thing, there was no good source of natural light. After examining the helixes and returning to them, I realized that the best pictures I could take in the Pillsbury A would be ones that documented and explored the many individual structures and objects that I found. In effect, I wanted to find the small stories that remained when the workers had left, and before the mill began to be transformed into a sophisticated new condominium complex.

Photographing James J. Hill's Great Northern Railway Office Building in the Lowertown section of St. Paul was a very different sort of experience. Designed by the architect James Brody, who was also the architect for Hill's Summit Avenue home, the Great Northern was built in 1887 in the Romanesque style favored by the Gilded Age's titans of industry. Occupying half a city block and seven stories tall, its large, arched entryway might have been part of a European castle. Even as the somewhat humbler center of Hill's railroad empire, given its U-shaped design, the Great Northern still had an interior courtyard where Hill watered his horse at an artesian spring.

Like the Pillsbury A, the Great Northern was constructed near the Mississippi in the heart of a busy industrial area, but the similarity ends there. When I encountered it, the Great Northern was like a lost soul. It had been put into retirement in the 1970's and no plans made for its future. Totally abandoned, over time it had become derelict. Vandals had stripped it of its marble fireplaces. Windows were shattered. The floors had buckled from rain and snow. There were the remains of small fires started for

73

warmth by vagrants. Wind howled through the broken out windows.

Though the Great Northern's early grandeur was thoroughly gone by the time I began to photograph it, I loved its condition. Sometimes I shot in black and white, but more often I used color to capture the effects of age and weather. There was a subtle depth of color in peeling paint or water-stained floors. I was also continually fascinated by the geometry of the huge, empty rooms. The Great Northern had been built with vaulted ceilings that had actual steel rails serving as beams, and its arched windows were immense. These intrinsic features of the building meant the scale and light were always exciting.

I worked in the Great Northern at different points over several years. After almost three decades of neglect, developers had started on a multi-year project to reclaim the building and convert it into lofts. This meant the space began to change as I worked. Debris was removed. Windows were restored. Once, when I arrived with an extremely wide-angle lens, I found that a section of vaulted ceiling had been removed by mistake. I set up my camera to capture a multi-story web of intersecting planes that became one of my favorite pictures from the entire project.

From the start of my work in the Pillsbury A, I knew I was recording something that had been preserved and was at a moment of transition. With the Great Northern, decay, and the particular character it created, became my subject. As work on the building began to transform it into new and modern spaces, I found that its eerie quality slowly disappeared. Today, the Great Northern has been saved from an untimely death by its renascence as lofts. By most standards, this is a good thing. Now, however, the building no longer draws my camera.

Pillsbury A Mill Flour Sifter

Pillsbury A Triple Machine

Great Northern Sixth Floor – Clean Open Space

Great Northern Fifth, Sixth, Seventh Floors

Great Northern Fireplace and Lines

Wells Fargo Spiral Staircase

Richard Beckham

Geriatria

Before retirement, hereafter known as BR, I spent hours on end in academic buildings on a small, midwestern public university campus. I had a modest office, space that I controlled myself. After years of working my way up the seniority ladder, my office even had a window offering a soothing view of a pine tree, greenery to spruce up the Wisconsin winter, and it faced west providing very nice afternoon light. Since I had worked in the Fine Arts Building for years, I knew intimately every classroom and, again, felt I had some control over my work space. Many hours, as a servant of bureaucracy, I spent in committee rooms of varying comfort and accommodation, but here too, as a senior faculty member who often chaired committees, I had some say about where and when we met, which enabled me to control some of my physical circumstances. All that was to change After Retirement.

AR acquainted me with some new spaces which for want of a better term I choose to call *geriatria*, spaces for "senior" citizens. Though I was no longer confined within the walls of public buildings, almost all of which might be described as Prison Modern, and though I now spent much time in my comfortable and well appointed home, I have come to know new spaces which are populated predominantly by older people, nay more accurately, very old people. Time is a factor in geriatria since some spaces function as such at certain times of the day only to transform themselves into places for all ages at others. Take the Lagoon and Edina Theaters in Minneapolis, for instance. The Lagoon, in the heart of the twenties-something scene in the Cities, usually attracts an audience varied in age, but in the afternoon all the young men and women are busy building careers so the movies are filled with hairless men and gray haired women. Or in River Falls, our local midwestern mecca of fine meals, The West Wind, appeals to people of all ages, but when you stop by for a late lunch or for the Friday night seafood buffet, you are again reminded that retirees have the time and affluence for leisurely dining.

But my awareness of geriatric gathering grounds grew after my wife Sue and I attended a couple of the Friday morning coffee concerts offered by the St. Paul Chamber Orchestra. Off and on for some years Sue and I have attended the evening concerts presented by this excellent orchestra. The crowd reflects the population at large, though younger children do not normally attend these affairs. But the audience is composed of a smattering of teenagers, more young adults, often exuding a serious and studious attitude which suggests they are music majors at one of the area colleges, a core of middle aged and prosperous men and women, and some older patrons.

Such a distribution does not hold true for the Coffee Concerts. While a couple of busloads of area school students are tucked discreetly away in some of the upper balcony seats and while all age groups are represented, the overwhelming majority of the audience is seniors. Friday outings work fine for those who have through retirement freed themselves of all other responsibilities and have the money and leisure to go to a public event at 10:30 in the morning.

In our travels in England Sue and I have often been struck by the term "Concessions," a word that when I first encountered it at the Duke's Playhouse in Lancaster I interpreted to mean that the Concessions admission price entitled one to the use of the bar, a requisite fixture of English theaters. It was only later that we fathomed that "Concessions" are discounted admissions offered to students, those on welfare, and the elderly. We cracked the code when we noticed the abbreviation "O. A. P." in the list of those eligible for Concessions and realized the theater admission cost less if you were an Old Age Pensioner.

We like the straightforwardness and accuracy of this term so much that we wish the "Coffee Concerts" could be renamed "O. A. P. Concerts," a more accurate description of the event. If you are not ready to do some field research on your own, I'll supply you with two examples of the impact senior citizens make when they descend on the Ordway for a morning fix of caffeine and Chopin.

Like the technologies that enable us to live longer, the technology of enabling people to move who have impaired mobility has made quantum leaps—pun intended. At the Ordway, the normally ambulatory patron is treated to a veritable display of mobility assistance devices. In contrast to the evening concerts where a person might see an occasional soul in a motorized conveyance, at the Coffee Concerts every fourth or fifth patron seems to use some device to aid walking or movement. You see plenty of simple canes, both traditional ones and the four-pronged model, but the more elaborate machines and devices seem to come at you from every angle. So many standard walkers appear with wheels on the front, a u-shaped frame, and skids on the rear covered with tennis balls, I'm almost persuaded that Spalding does a brisker business supplying balls for walkers than it does for tennis players.

Those for whom such walkers are no longer adequate ride motorized carts or wheel chairs in a variety of sleek and functional designs. And some of the drivers of these vehicles are convinced that their need for mobility assistance gives them right of way over ordinary and lowly pedestrians. For a brief moment on each of our morning visits to the Ordway I have an anxiety attack prompted by the feeling that I am being beset on all sides by canes, walkers, carts and wheelchairs. In spite of the traffic flow problems this fleet of mobility devices creates, I do take comfort in the fact that Medicare will help pay for my "Rover" when the time comes that I need it.

Having hashed over the mobility challenged, I will choose a broader group for my second example: men. It's the perennial bathroom issue with a twist. For decades frequenters of public places have known that the architects, working in a historically male dominated profession, built a gender bias into their buildings—too few restrooms for women. At Northrup Auditorium, for example, women almost always have to line up out into the hall in order to use the facilities, while next door men never need to wait for a urinal to come open. Perhaps the Friday morning restroom situation at the Ordway is nature finally getting even with men for designing inadequate restroom facilities for women.

It is a fact universally recognized that many older men are victims of prostate disorders. The consequences become immediately clear when you go to the men's room on Coffee Concert days, especially since coffee is a well known diuretic. Smirk if you wish, women, but lines form in the men's room. As enlarged prostates narrow the urethra, men find it harder to start and once started even more difficult to finish emptying the bladder. Add to that the subtle pressure a person feels when he is standing in front of the urinal doing nothing even though the urge is distinctly there and lines of fellow sufferers are patiently waiting behind him, and you get some sense of the dimension of the problem. Many a man turns away mission unaccomplished under the stress of these conditions. Many a concerto virtuoso or brilliant orchestral interpretation of a symphony goes not fully appreciated after intermission because the listener still needs a pee. Enough focus on the urinary tract. Let us now focus on the body as a whole.

I read a while back about a British woman who sued the university she worked for because sitting in long meetings caused her to develop deep vein thrombosis. I'm not surprised, but I am happy that in spite of spending decades in long meetings I escaped into retirement relatively unscathed. But to stay that way as an O. A. P. requires some effort, so Sue and I have become active at the River Falls Area Hospital Wellness Center. Unlike the Ordway Coffee Concerts, the Wellness Center is not an overwhelmingly geriatric institution, but its population is skewed toward older people. As with the coffee concerts, the elders tend to play in the mornings when the young are at work. This center has an excellent staff, almost exclusively women in their late twenties or early thirties, who are always ready to help with an exercise program or with the complicated machinery used in it. But the Center is not solely a place to work out. It's also an important social site.

It's natural that retirees should congregate at the Wellness Center. They have the time, money and energy to try to keep declining physiques functioning. And some of the internees in the Wellness Center came there from the adjacent Rehabilitation Clinic where they were sent to rehab joints either out of sync or out of the body and replaced by artificial ones. Given this gathering of older citizens and the social impetus of the place, old body builders focus much of their conversation on the center of attention for the elderly: their bodies. A free flowing forum on medications, treatments, procedures, and exercises is constantly in progress. The staff works hard to enable. "You have atrial fib. Why don't you talk to Betsy? She has it too and may have some tips for you. It hits her so hard she can't function when it comes on." As a retired colleague recently observed, "We used to get together and talk about university politics or the state of the world. Now all our conversations center on what medications we are on and what the dosage is." If you don't have a symptom and want to chat with the person on the next treadmill, you'd better make one up.

Gender circumstances here are quite different from those at the Ordway. In the men's locker room, since the group is quite small, there is none of the pressure to perform and return to the fray. But it is a locker room and inevitably brings back memories of past athletic glory. The conversations which such memories engender lead ex-jocks to try to recapture verbally the ecstasy of triumphs past. Left waiting outside, the women can do little but commiserate and complain. Inside the men make one more stab at recalling youth and vigor.

All in all both men and women here are pampered lots. The young women on staff relate easily to the women, no doubt because they both respect their efforts to stay physically able and because they know some day they will probably be doing the same. The men exercise that coy flirtatiousness that older men practice on younger women, both groups knowing full well that age has kicked these guys out of the game. In one way the Wellness Center is a sobering place given that you see there people who come to recover from major cardiac events and hip or knee replacements. It's a reminder of possibilities that lie ahead for the recently retired. But in another way it is a joyful place. The participants appreciate the strength and mobility they have and want to keep and the tone of their conversations and interactions reflect a sense that good health is a grace to be appreciated.

The geriatrium where age seems most to enclose me is the St. Paul Heart Clinic. Over the last few months a recurrent problem with atrial fibrillation led to a series of tests which showed that I also needed angioplasty and stents. In my several visits to the heart clinic I don't recall seeing anyone there for treatment who was younger than fifty, and more likely the patients seemed to be in their sixties, seventies and even eighties. While I was preparing for the exercise part of my nuclear imaging stress test I got a glimpse of the elderly woman just behind me in the process. She was in her eighties, walking with a cane and stooped with age. Yet here she was having a heart problem diagnosed. For many people it is obvious that a lifetime of living takes a toll on this important muscle which functions twenty-four hours a day.

While, if I had had a choice, I would prefer not to join this age-driven group, I feel blessed by the astonishing technology available to it.

The nuclear imaging stress test essentially involves injecting two types of radioactive material into the blood stream—one before and one after exercise—and taking a series of x-ray pictures of the heart. It's easy to be amused by the effects since for a month afterwards people taking the test and flying outside the country must take along documentation to explain to the U. S. Customs officials why they set off Geiger counters on return. Even more astonishing is the ability cardiologists have to identify blockages in coronary arteries through inserting dye into the heart, to remove those blockages through angioplasty, and to keep the arteries open by placing stents. All this the surgeon accomplishes with two valium tablets and a local anesthetic at the point where the catheters are inserted. At St. Paul Heart Clinic the staff appears to be young and vigorous. It's just as well, given that the procedures done there require a steady hand, an accurate eye, a quick mind and a thorough knowledge of medical technology.

BR, Before Retirement, I was not exactly a "couch potato," but neither was I diligent about cardiovascular exercise. Now AR, such exercise is no longer a desideratum, it's a necessity. Since my visit to the "Cath Lab" at St. Paul Heart Clinic, my participation in the Wellness Center program has taken on new significance. The timely discovery and treatment of my coronary artery disease gives me an obligation to see that I do what I can to keep the pump going. That includes daily cardiovascular exercise, medications, and renewed attention to a heart-healthy diet. Also it gives me a whole new vocabulary of symptoms, treatments and medications. No longer am I limited to "A Fib" as a condition I must deal with. I can now talk authoritatively about absence of symptoms as a symptom, about the "Cath Lab," and about rat poison as a blood thinner.

I know eventually I will probably arrive at that final stage of old agedness when I enter a residential care center like the one down the street from our house, the Lutheran Home, the name of which is decidedly post-modern given that it in no way resembles a "home." I hope I will adjust to that geriatrium as I have to others. In the meantime, though, I intend to walk the walk, often on the treadmill at the Wellness Center, and to talk the talk in the locker room there.

Carol Dolphin

Monochromatic Prism

As I grow older,
The world seems grayer to me –
Not in dreary shades of dullness and depression
But in dove-toned hues of blended softness.

Vanished are the screaming absolutes of black & white,
The powerful closers of "yes" and "no,"
As "usually" replaces "always"
And "never" is tempered by "seldom."

It's freeing, this grayness,
With a willingness to see others as they are
Without the recriminations of right or wrong
Or the slamming doors of judgment.

It's color-filled, this grayness,
A rainbow of newness in undiscovered worlds,
With values and lifestyles which may not be mine
But which I can see as yours and good for you.
It's peaceful, this grayness,
It takes less energy to accept than to reject
To remain open instead of resisting entry
To trade acceptance for cynicism, distrust, hate.

Yes, I am getting older (Is it possible – retired even?)
But in <u>this</u> grayness – at least – I can be comfortable
And never – better make that seldom –
Want to go back.

David McCordick

The Priest, The Angel, and The AIDS Test[2]

> *Old age hath yet his honor and his toil.*
> Alfred Lord Tennyson

A major problem with retirement, of course, is the other retired people one encounters. Other retired people like to tell stories. Each story that you listen to will kill about fifty thousand brain cells. There are three categories of story that are especially painful:

A. Have I told you lately about my grandchildren?
B. Have I told you lately about our trip to Bermuda?
C. Have I told you lately about my colonoscopy?
Well, this is the colonoscopy one.

Like Homer, I have divided my epic into books. There are four books in this particular case. The first is "The Last Rites"; the second, "The March of the Enemas—José and the Angel"; the third, "I'm Afraid We've Had a Little Accident—the AIDS Test"; and the fourth, "Aladdin's Cave". There is an addendum: "Something for the Neighbors."

Book I: The Last Rites

My story begins in a doctor's office. My doctor is a round-bodied sleek-faced East Indian fellow who does not look at you

---

[2] The following is a piece of oral history, taped by the author in a single sitting, without interruption and without notes.

when he talks to you. Presumably he is embarrassed at the shape you are in, not to mention the shape he is in. He asked me if my father is deceased and I say that he is and I add, because doctors like to know these things, that my father died of colon cancer. His face lights up; his dark eyes gleam.

"Ah," he says, "we have learned a great deal about colon cancer. Now we treat it aggressively."

When he says "aggressively" an image passes across my mind of Green Bay Packers training camps. I am confused but I nod.

"You must have a colonoscopy."

"Aha," I say. "What's that?"

"It is a procedure," he says. "We insert a tube into the lower part of your abdomen and at the end of this tube is a camera and a light. The camera passes all the way through your intestines. It takes a picture of your entire colon, which is shown on a screen that the doctor is watching, and the doctor can see what he needs to see—polyps for example. There's a little pair of scissors attached to this instrument and the doctor can cut out the polyp he sees and send it to the lab for investigation."

When he describes the wondrous tube with the camera another image passes across my mind—one of those great black outdoor electrical conduits that one encounters at Christmas time with one of those old-fashioned 35 mm Minolta cameras attached to the end snaking its way through my intestines, the camera twitching eagerly like a maniacal peeping-tom looking to the right, to the left.

The doctor sees I am looking a little horrified: "It doesn't hurt," he says.

"Ah," I say.

Subsequent to this I find myself in the waiting room of the hospital. I am one of many in the room, in various degrees of physical debility, looking shyly about us, not making eye contact, reading ancient copies of the *Readers Digest*, waiting for our name to be called. Nurses come to the door and they call out, always by a first name—George, Bill, Evelyn. It's a command, of course, but it's also an inquiry and it's a re-affirmation somehow of your humanity. Someone stands up and walks proudly, perhaps shamblingly and he and the nurse disappear together for their mutual gratification into the interior of the cubicles.

I wait for this. My name is David. The nurse comes and she calls out to the room: "David," and I am rather proud. I put my magazine down and I hoist myself to my feet. People around me look at me with some approval, but as I start to move toward the lady I realize with some horror she is not looking at me. She's looking at another person and smiling at him and he, a somewhat older man than I, is smiling at her. They come together at the doorway and turn like a couple, not arm in arm but in serious propinquity, into the interiors.

I am embarrassed; I am ashamed; I sit back down. People around me do not look at me. Clearly I have been trying to pass myself off as David. There's no point in telling them I am David. Clearly I am the wrong David. I sit in embarrassed silence. Time passes. Others are called; others take their places in seats. Finally another nurse appears, looks about her. "David," she says. For a moment I look about me; no one has moved. I stand up quietly, modestly I would say, and I join this lady. She looks at me a shade this side of indifferently.

"Come with me," she says, and I do.

She takes me into one of those rooms. I am disrobed; my things disappear into a cubicle somewhere. I am given one of those impossible back-ass-ward gowns and the cute little booties. The floors are cold. I sit there in solitude. Someone in a white coat comes and takes me out of this room into another room and goes away without explanation or comment. In this room there are two stools. There is nothing else. There is not even a chart, an eye, or a pancreas on the walls—just two stools in a small room—a consulting room. I sit there in my booties and my gown.

The door opens; I look up. Surely this is the doctor; it is not. It is a man older than I dressed in black. I realize with a shock he is wearing a clerical collar. He has in his hand a clipboard with a yellow pad of some kind. Almost certainly my name, David, is written on this pad. He comes toward me, hands out; we shake hands.

"I am Father X," he says. (I have made up this name.) "And I have come to talk to you. I hope you don't mind. You certainly don't have to talk to me, but I—I'd like to talk to you. It's all right if you're not a Catholic; I see that you have checked no religion on your admission sheet and that's perfectly all right. I'm not here to try to proselytize, but simply to talk to you for a few minutes. Would that be all right?"

"Well, yes, it would be all right." I'm actually rather pleased—confused. This has not happened to me in a hospital before, but I'm rather pleased.

So we talk. He tells me that God loves me. This too is good news. He says that God will not judge me harshly, that God, in fact, is rooting for me. He understands that people sin; that no one leads a perfect life and it is only necessary that we be ready, that we feel we have cleansed ourselves.

I am beginning to worry about my colonoscopy. I had been advised that it was not hurtful. I suspected that it was embarrassing; there was even the possibility that it was disgusting, but clearly God was involved, and it was beginning to look serious.

He must have judged by the glum look on my face that he had made perhaps the wrong impression, and he assured me there was nothing to be alarmed about: "We just like to talk for a few minutes. I—I talk to people who are going in for these kinds of operations. I'm not proselytizing or asking you to join anything or pray with me, but just talk for a few minutes so that when you go into that room you're in a state of readiness, and you'll know that God is on your side. The operation will surely be fine. Many, many of these operations are quite, quite successful. But if—if things don't go well you're at peace, and that's just very important."

"I'm—having a colonoscopy," I said.

"You're having a colonoscopy?" he said.

"Yes."

"No—you're having heart surgery." He looked at his yellow pad. "Your name is David?"

"Yes, it is."

"Aren't you having heart surgery?"

"Nope."

"Having a colonoscopy. That's where they put this tube up your . . . where they put this tube?"

"Yes."

He looked at his pad again in some confusion. "Well," he said hopefully, "colonoscopies can be dangerous too; it's an operation . . ."

"No, it's not an operation," I said, "It's a procedure. They just put this . . . it's not . . . it's not got anything. . ." Then I thought about the scissors and the Minolta, and then I thought, well, perhaps he knows.

"Well," said the priest, Father X, "there has been . . . I think there has been some mistake. Well, I have enjoyed very much talking to you."

"Oh, yes, thank you," I said. "I enjoyed talking to you."

"I think there has been a mistake. I'll have to talk to someone. Well, thank you very much, David."

We shook hands and he left. By this time I had worked it out. The other David was surely having a colonoscopy in some room, a few feet away from where we stood. Perhaps this surprised him. I, on the other hand, was perhaps only a few minutes away from open heart surgery. And, no doubt being wheeled into the place under anesthetics, I would not have noticed one way or the other. That's enough to make one nervous. Well, at least I had learned that God forgives sins, and that he was on my side and that's something. I sat there, rather expecting the priest to come back and explain, but he did not.

Book II: The March of the Enemas – José and the Angel

Instead, the door opened after a while and a fellow who looked vaguely Hispanic walked in. He looked at me: "My name is José," he said, "and I'm going to give you an enema."

"Uh," I said.

"It doesn't hurt," he said.

"Well," I said, "I've been fasting for two days. I haven't had any solid food . . ."

"Doesn't hurt."

"And I've drunk gallons of that stuff they give you at the pharmacy that tastes awful and it's almost certain I don't need . . ."

"It doesn't hurt," he said. "I'm very good at it. You come with me. It's hospital procedure. We must do this and have an enema."

"Okay," I said.

I went with José. We came into a room which had a table that I was obviously to lie upon, and next to it was an abnormally large and, it seemed to me, very pristine toilet. Well, there's no need—is there?—to go into the procedure. José did not speak very good English; he had very little of what the British call small talk, but there was one phrase which he could speak with alarming clarity and with a saint-like doggedness: "You can take some more."

"No, no."

"You can take some more."

"No, no."

"You can take some more."

When it was over I was exhausted, empty, a little embarrassed, shaking. José, sad-faced and even I should say sour-faced, led me back. Was I distasteful to him? Was this job distasteful to him? Did he start out in the enema section and work up from there? At any rate, I was taken to another room and there I waited.

Well, then the door opened again, and something astonishing walked in. An apparition. An Angel. An extraordinarily beautiful woman—slender—one of those perfect slender figures you see from time to time, looking incredibly fetching in her nurse's uniform. I like to remember her as a blonde but it is entirely possible that she merely had very light brown hair. After all, she was wearing a cap of some kind. She had an angelic smile.

"Are you ready for our enema?" she said.

"Oh, no," I said.

She smiled, "It doesn't hurt."

"No, no—no, no. I had an enema."

"Well, yes, of course you have, but we have to give you one here in the hospital."

"No, no; no, no, I had . . . I've had an enema right here in the hospital."

"I give very good enemas. It will all be over . . . I have a lot of experience—never lost a patient yet."

"Uh, no. No, no—you don't understand. I've had an enema right here in the hospital, just a few minutes ago."

"Oh, surely not. I'm to give you your enema. It says right here. Your name is David?"

"Yes, yes, but—José, the Puerto Rican—well, maybe he's Mexican—anyway, he gave me an enema right here—well, I mean over there—just a few minutes ago."

"I'm supposed to give you an enema. José is not supposed to give you an enema. He has no business giving you an enema."

"Well, I'm sorry."

Her eyes became hopeful for a moment: "Well, I don't suppose . . .

93

"No, no, no, one enema's enough, honest."

She frowned at me: "Well, I'll have to talk to someone about this. This ought not to be happening."

You have no idea how badly I felt for her. I had never been this close to an angel. I had come within a hair of what can only be described as a highly intimate experience with an angel. But then she had turned and she was gone.

"I'll be back," she said. I knew she would not and indeed she did not come back.

After a while another person whom I had not seen, also wearing a white smock, came and took me into the colonoscopy room. At this point I was prepared for anything. It had been one of those days.

Book III: I'm Afraid We've Had a Little Accident—the AIDS Test

They put me on a bed next to a television set which was on, but showing just a white picture. Nurses fussed about me. One of them gave me a shot which she said was a relaxant.

"This is not supposed to anesthetize you," she said, "but it probably will. It means you won't feel anything but I'm almost certain this will put you to sleep; it puts most people to sleep."

Nothing puts me to sleep. I do not sleep on planes; I do not sleep on buses, trains; I do not sleep. I knew I would be bolt awake during the operation, such as it was, but she smiled so I smiled. She went away. Another nurse came and she stabbed me with something; that too was fine. I was actually relaxing because this is the part of the hospital that seemed comfortable—except that a fussy little man came in the door and he had an odd look on his face.

"I'm sorry," he said, "but there's been an accident. We're going to have to test you for AIDS."

Now you must judge the effect this had on me. "There's been an accident and I'll have to test you for AIDS." Well, I'll be damned. I've got AIDS. It's that damned enema guy; he didn't wash his hands.

"How could I have AIDS?" I said.

"Well," he said, "the explanation is simply that one of our nurses—she is a little embarrassed about this so she has sent me in to explain this to you—has stabbed herself with the needle she just took out of you. Now this happens from time to time."

This was news to me, you appreciate, that nurses stab themselves with needles on a regular basis.

"But," he said, "our, uh, hospital procedures are such that when this does happen the patient must be tested for AIDS."

"But," I said, "I don't have that kind of lifestyle. There's just no possib. . ."

"It doesn't hurt," he says.

"But I really only have the one partner and she . . ."

"It doesn't, it doesn't hurt and we—we don't charge for this. Now, it's entirely voluntary; you actually have to sign. I've got—I've brought the agreement with me. You'll have to sign this piece of paper giving us permission to do this, but we must do this—we really must."

Of course I agreed. Why not, I thought. I've learned the ways of God to man. I have been saved from heart surgery. I have been offered two enemas for the price of one. Why shouldn't I get a free AIDS test? So the test was taken.

Book IV: Aladdin's Cave

The colonoscopist—is that what one calls him, a colonoscopist?— came in. A youngish fellow, chipper, quite cheerful as a matter of fact, leaned me over on my side: "We're going to have to get you comfortable," he said.

Actually I had been comfortable, but he leaned me on one side. No one could be comfortable lying on his elbow.

"Now, you just lay there."

I wanted to explain to him that that particular use of the word, lay, applied only to fornicators or to chickens, but it seemed an inappropriate time to do this. He was being so cheerful and so professional, and nobody likes an English teacher. So I took the position.

"You'll be off to sleep in a minute," he said. "That's usually what happens, but if you're around for the first few minutes you might be interested in watching the television set, because in a minute it will start to show the inside of your intestine. Now just hang on for a minute here."

So he inserted the object into the lower part of the abdomen and, sure enough, Aladdin's cave appeared, magnificently colored—blues, reds and oranges, no stalactites, no stalagmites, no bats—looking rather pristine. It—it looked, in fact, rather beautiful—some wonderful natural object like the Painted Desert or the Grand Canyon early in the morning.

"You're not asleep," he said to me. "I don't think you're going to sleep."

"No."

"Well, may as well enjoy this then. This part is the . . . ," and so on and so forth. He began discussing where we were and what he was looking for. I was awed.

"It's not as interesting as it might be," he said, "because we have no polyps. If we had polyps it would be more interesting. We would stop; we would snip one or two of the polyps. That's always very interesting, but you have no polyps."

"I have no polyps."

"Right. You have no polyps."

"Does this mean I have no cancer?"

"Almost certainly. You are polyp-less."

Well, I was rather pleased. You can understand that I would be rather pleased. We moved slowly and, I should say beautifully, through the entire intestine which is quite a long thing, apparently, wrapped up on itself as it is until we got to the end. He had to tell me that it was the end; there were no exit signs as you might guess.

"So," he said, "this is all just wonderful. We're going to give you a clean bill of health."

Having said that he then pulled the tube out. I say this in this rather flat way. The going up the intestine was a slow and artful business; he was paying a great deal of attention to it, of course. But now he had seen everything that his Minolta had to show and so pulling the tube out was simply a thing to be done without paying any attention. I mention this to you only because the sight of one's intestines going by on one's TV set at full speed was, well, a little sickening. I was thrown slightly, but all in all it worked out well. After a short while I was minus my booties, minus my gown, in the car, home, and able to eat.

Addendum: Something for the Neighbors

Two weeks later, the phone rang and an extraordinarily exuberant voice on the other side said: "You don't have AIDS."

"I don't have AIDS," I say.

"Yes. Your name is David?"

"Yes, yes."

"Well, you don't have AIDS. That's the test—it's negative. Congratulations."

"Thank you," I said.

Now, there was no chance I could have AIDS. Nonetheless, I felt relieved. I felt I had won something. And I rather wanted to go and tell the neighbors that I didn't have AIDS. But I thought about that and I had the feeling that if I had gone up and down my neighborhood calling into the doors and windows: "Hey, good news—I don't have AIDS," I would not produce the effect that I might have hoped.

And this is my colonoscopy story. And, say, have I told you about my trip to Bermuda?

Travel

Our happiest moments as tourists always seem to come when we stumble upon one thing while in pursuit of something else.

Lawrence Block

Sue Bridwell Beckham

Playing House on a Small Island

"If I could go on all these trips, I'd want to go to a lot of different countries—not the same ones over and over?" It was a question despite its declarative structure, and it was my daughter-in-law speaking. My husband Dick and I had just returned from about our ninth trip to England in a dozen years. We had spent thirty-one days in England: two weeks in London, a few days in Yorkshire very near the Lake District where we have been many times, a few more days in Lincolnshire and a week in Cornwall, first time visits for the last two. During the time we have kept returning to the United Kingdom, we have visited other, more exotic places: China, Mexico, Turkey, Italy three times and Greece twice, Spain, Canada, the Blue Grass music country of Appalachia, the Grand Canyon and Yellowstone, Florida even.

We've traveled much in recent years, and now that we've retired, travel has become the locus about which we structure the rest of our lives—the volunteer work, the family, our lives with our cats. Still the world is full of countries that we haven't visited, some of which we haven't even considered. And it is full of more adventurous destinations than England, Scotland or even Cornwall. But at the slightest hint of an opportunity, we return to England and Scotland. And often, we return to favorite spots in those nations; we joke that we'll require that our ashes be scattered in the Lake District so that our children will be forced to walk in that enchanted land.

So back to my daughter-in-law—why do we visit England so often and Venezuela and Thailand not at all? The partially shared language doesn't hurt, although it's not such a great help as one would imagine. There are so many English speakers everywhere that it is often embarrassing to be mostly mono-lingual.

And so many so-called English locutions are not so shared as they seem: our Lancaster friend Sue Bloxham, with whom we took this trip's Lake District walks, had great difficulty with our use of the word "town." In our presence, she amusedly told her friend that "They call everything a town even if it has only a store, a pub and a few houses." We explained that in the States, except maybe New England, the word *village* is an affectation.

One probable reason we return repeatedly to England is that between us we have five degrees in English, one in American Studies and a history of teaching and reading English literature. By the time we visited England the first time in 1970 we were already old friends with that country. At last, that which we had studied became rock solid. We loved seeing where Beowulf might have fought Grendel, where the Wife of Bath told her risqué tale, where Elizabeth may have been courted by Darcy and where Heathcliff and Catherine still wander the moors keening for lost love and life. We love to walk where Wordsworth walked— twenty-four miles in the rugged and rocky, but not forested, Lake District on his seventieth birthday—to sup chocolate where Dr. Johnson may have regaled Boswell, and we love to see the dwellings of long dead monarchs.

But that accounts for only part of it. Those charms have waned with familiarity to be replaced with more subtle but more gripping ones and we still keep returning. I cannot speak for Dick, but I've come up with a theory for why I keep returning to England and Scotland. I have loved playing house for well over sixty years now. It started when my mother designated a corner of her kitchen, about a four foot square, as my kitchen. I was named Ida Sue then—it was Ida Sue's Kitchen. Mother furnished it with a tiny stove that really worked, although, with no heat regulator, it usually burned my biscuits and cookies; a tiny sink with a tank that could be filled, and a spigot that ran drips of water. She gave me the tools to bake: a minuscule rolling pin, a dough board, a tiny egg beater, pots and even a tube pan. My infatuation with the miniature probably started there in that contained, tiny, but functional kitchen. I still love playing house and I still love the miniature, the compact, the creative use of small space.

You see the real attraction of the United Kingdom for me seems to be one of scale. Whatever can be said of our nation both good and bad, it can never be considered small in any way. The land, the wealth, the impact and the mistakes are all huge. England

and Scotland[3], on the other hand, comprise what Bill Bryson has designated a "small island." Even so, in terms of history, diversity, generosity of spirit, grace, contribution to the world of ideas—and mistakes—that island is at least as big as our nation. And all of it is much more accessible because the scale is less, because it is dense, it is compact. The United States is much, much larger (including Alaska nearly 6,000,000 square miles) than the United Kingdom (94,525 square miles when Northern Ireland is counted) and has more spectacular geography. And yet, that tiny island that is England, Scotland and Wales, has a variety at least as great; because the variety is more subtle, it is more certain and, one hopes, because it does not so obviously invite commercial interference, more durable.

Before going on, I must pay tribute to my favorite miniature but grand British place. The Lake District is a study in small scale, great impact, and resistance to alteration. Our first adventure this trip was walking in the Lake District with Sue Bloxham as guide, instead of following the *Walks in the Lake District* books we usually use. After several weeks of rain, we slogged in the muck—when I returned one day caked with Lake District clay, the other Sue dubbed me a "mucky pup." But the walks were exhilarating; one day, the sun came out just in time for our lunch beside a cascading brook and in sight of a spectacular falls. Dick and I think the Smoky Mountains are the closest the U.S. has to the Lake District both in spectacular hiking and in the population's love for it. And, next to the Lake District, that's where we get our souls revived. But the Smokies are much larger.

The four highest peaks in the United Kingdom don't reach 3,300 feet and all of them are in the Lake District. The Lake District itself is about forty to forty-five miles across in any direction and yet, it is the favorite walking area in England, if not the world. The tiny area is so riddled with cliffs, waterfalls, surprising twists of land and turns of water that many more modern people than Wordsworth have made walking "in the Lakes" a primary goal in life. Sue Bloxham was very disappointed that in the three days we spent visiting, we didn't make a Lake

---

[3] Wales figures little in this essay because I haven't traveled much in Wales and, as fascinating as its history and language is, it doesn't very often show up in my fantasies about where I'd like to be.

District "walk" of more than eight and a half miles. But there will be a next time.

Walking is a traditional English pastime, a vacation destination in itself. To see the English and Scottish variety, to appreciate that island, to wish for repeat trips, one just needs to look closer, and to do that, one needs to walk. Recently, I was walking in Wisconsin with my friend Ruth on a walk that went three miles in one direction and three miles back along the same path—because in the States, we have not devised easily accessible circle walks and then published books to help people follow them as they have in England. While we walked, we discussed our trips to England, as we often do. Ruth mentioned a particularly delightful sojourn in the Cotswolds. I confessed that I had never been there. "What?" she exclaimed, "You have never been to the Cotswolds! You must go." And on she went. England is no larger than the area of our country destroyed by Hurricane Katrina, and yet I had not been to one of its prime vacation spots! In fact, the UK is not much larger than our home state of Wisconsin and yet, with all our exploration, we've only recently visited small portions of two of its major counties and that's not all; we plan to visit them again as soon as we can because there was so much we didn't see. When can I find time to visit the Cotswolds with so much of Cornwall and Lincolnshire yet to explore?

On this trip, after the Lake District, it was in Lincolnshire where we walked and played house. As you've noticed, I do love to play house. This trip offered ample opportunity to do that. We stayed in three "self-catering" cottages during this month; two of them were typically British compact. I guess Dick and I no longer think of England in terms of its ostentatious manor houses, palaces and museums. Those palaces are scattered in the wooded areas (because ancient dukes preserved the woods for their own hunting while they let the populace denude the rest of the island for building materials and firewood), but the people and the romance of that island for us lives small and close together. It isn't just the area covered by this country that is small by American standards. Probably because they live on a small island, the Brits are accustomed to smaller distance, smaller personal space, smaller "villages," smaller stores, smaller "gardens" (yards to us), smaller cars and smaller kitchens.

The first cottage we rented on this trip was a Landmark Trust site that had a kitchen little larger than Ida Sue's kitchen in

Cynthiana, Kentucky, sixty years ago. The Landmark Trust is a very un-American organization devoted to saving and making use of antique properties not quite important enough to become museums. With foundation money, individual donations, and proceeds from renting properties—as well as a great deal of determination and commitment—the Landmark Trust restores and revitalizes charming, historic buildings that have been nearly lost to neglect.

The "Chateau" near Gainsborough, Lincolnshire, is such a property. The present owners of a large estate dating back centuries had neither use nor need for an eighteenth-century building in a state of collapse. Thus, they ceded the building with a bit of woods around it to the Landmark Trust just before it would have crumbled beyond restoration. The building itself was miniature. Two and a half centuries ago, the young city dwelling owner of the property decided that his country land would be a great place to spend the occasional weekend. So he built a retreat. The result was the tiniest "manor house" one can imagine. So far as Landmark Trust research has been able to determine, he built the two-story place for himself and the servants he needed for a weekend now and then. The first floor was his, the ground floor for the servants. Landmark Trust saved the building and its aura but redesigned it in such a way that two to three people—probably only English people accustomed to fitting a globally renowned culture onto a small island would find the sleeping arrangements adequate for three—could sleep there for a holiday.

Outside, the Chateau does indeed look like a manor house with classical lines, elegant lintels and cornices, wings at either end—except after the thick walls are subtracted, the wings will hardly hold a bed apiece. Inside, it is exquisitely decorated with gorgeous white woodwork replicated from similar places three hundred years ago. The first floor has a single room roughly fifteen foot square used as lounge, parlor, living room, whatever Brits and Americans choose to call it. In it are a drop leaf game table, a sofa, fresh flowers (when it's rented), two small chests, an open fire place and several modest chairs.

Just off this room, one wing perhaps seven by seven is the bedroom. In it fits a double bed crunched up against the wall on one side with barely space enough to walk beside it on the other. On that side is a diminutive bedside table and a small lamp. In the other wing has been added the interior winding stairway (the seventeenth-century occupants had to move between the floors on the outside) and a small book shelf with publications about walks in this part of Lincolnshire, books of Lincolnshire fiction and poetry, the guest book with tips on where to eat and where to walk—a tiny library for a tiny house and its guests.

Note the emphasis on walking literature. We go to England because we can still walk and most people there choose to. One determinant always about where we choose to stay is where we can walk. DWI laws are stringent in the UK, so one wants to make sure there's a pub within a mile or so. Like many Brits, we like to walk to the bakery for our bread and scones, to the butcher for absolutely fresh meat, to the green grocer, to the post office. For recreation or utility, walking is sacred in the UK. Ancient footpaths must be preserved and must be open to the peripatetic public to the extent that when a motorway (like our interstates) must cross a traditional footpath, a footbridge is built across it. One of our sad discoveries on this most recent trip is that open pathways are under fire by some property owners. On ancient paths, we found new stiles that were very difficult to cross, occasional illegal fences across the path leaving just enough space to squeeze under, and some unfriendly signs threatening us if we did not keep to the marked path. But those were few and, in the summer of 2004, dedicated British walkers organized a nationwide "hike" that involved volunteers covering every footpath on the island to make sure each one was open to the public. Even so, Dick and I found a couple of new fences—clearly built after the walk—close enough to the path to make passage difficult.

The Chateau was well situated for walks although the shop in the village about a mile down the road had recently succumbed to more distant supermarket competition. And it was well suited to a compact holiday. Down the spiral stairway, on the ground floor, is the kitchen with the typical British refrigerator (not much larger than we give our children to take to college but of much better quality), the typical four-burner British stove (*not* a grandiose "cooker" such as middle class Brits with a taste for tradition might have in their homes), a small sink and enough small cookware to cook for two—or four if you must.[4] One could

---

[4] In Low Bentham, Yorkshire, we visited friends who had restored a seventeenth-century farmhouse. Their kitchen was the size of a small American kitchen and had a small American style refrigerator, but this

make most anything on a small scale in that kitchen. Although the dishes were new, they were chosen to fit into a splendid period residence; they matched, they were elegantly shaped, and there were enough to serve four, the greatest number Landmark Trust permits even to visit the house at one time.

That's one corner of the ground floor. A second corner has a built-in breakfast nook with benches against two walls and possibly enough space to accommodate chairs for two guests. The third corner is occupied by the toilet room elegantly furnished with fine porcelain fixtures and window sills about twenty-four inches thick, and the fourth is the bathroom—a tub and a second porcelain washbasin. Between is a broom closet. That's it, except the second bedroom. Downstairs under the upper bedroom, it is the same size but with a single bed, thus permitting a third occupant—we chose to sleep separately for comfort—and space for a small chest to store clothes in.

The Chateau was charming and it was perfect for playing house. We "journaled." We worked jigsaw puzzles. We figured out how to store our clothes with virtually no storage space; we listened to birds and enjoyed the tiny woods—a small sign asked that we not walk in the woods during nesting season—but it was October, and we leaned on the period fence to see the River Trent just a few acres across the landlords' land. I cooked simple meals with free range eggs, grass fed beef, local sausage, locally grown kale and tomatoes, all available in the Gainsborough markets.

A week or so before at a farmers' market in High Bentham, I had remarked that the beef was grass fed. The aforementioned Sue Bloxham patiently explained that "it is all grass fed here." What made the labeled beef remarkable was that the grass it fed on was grown just a few miles from High Bentham on Ingleborough, a favorite "walking" mountain of Benthamites—for Brits pleasure is walking even if it is twelve miles over mountains—a hike, on the other hand, is work.

The Brits assume that their food will be locally grown, or, in the case of citrus, flown in from Spain. They assume that

---

couple consider themselves continental. We also visited people in Lowth, Lincolnshire, who had a new upscale house and a large, by English standards, kitchen (perhaps 15 x 17). These were both considered *atypical* residences and, in both cases, the owners were proud that their kitchens did not look like British kitchens.

grazing animals actually graze for their food, that other livestock are fed as they have been for centuries and not gorged with some chemical mixture designed for unnaturally rapid growth. When they think about it, they want traditional food—no Monsanto, no ADM. The sad part is that increasingly they don't think about it. The supermarket movement and, as in the United States, the increased need for both adults in a family to work outside the home, have meant that the Brits look less at what's in what they eat and more at how quickly it can be prepared. One can find chemically and genetically modified food in the United Kingdom. But not so much as here. It seems that at the very least, half the produce and pre-packaged food even on supermarket shelves carries a trustworthy organic label or a guarantee that the animal was free range. And very few unintelligible additives are listed on labels.

But perhaps too much editorializing. Lincolnshire has more attractions than locally grown food. While we never avoid a cathedral that stares us in the face, Dick and I have found visiting centuries-old parish churches to be more satisfying. We did visit Lincoln Cathedral and we did take the "roof tour." Where else can you see the top side of gothic vaults? the gigantic timbers cut while there were still first growth trees in Britain? and the re-placement timbers donated by an earl after the 1987 "hurricane" took down fifteen million of England's remaining trees? Incidentally, timbers from trees blown down in that same hurricane make up the infrastructure of the new Globe Theatre in London. But only in Lincoln Cathedral can you walk through the top arch of a flying buttress and stare at the city below with a student who says, "That's my house over there!" Still, the parish church in the Lincolnshire city of Lowth has the tallest non-cathedral spire in the United Kingdom, and we took nearly as much pleasure walking to its top.

At the Chateau, we cooked, played, wrote and talked. And in the day, we went out to walk. I love to play house. But even more, I do love to walk. When we first went to England thirty-five years ago, we tried exploring by train, but from the train window I kept seeing wee signs labeling "public footpath to . . ." I longed to take a public footpath, to walk from one town to another in a space designed for walking, one that had evolved because it was the proper route for a footpath. So today, we plan our trips to walk. The best walks—even in the Lake District where the object is to end one's ramble at a legendary pub—lead from one village through a couple more, where we stop to investigate the parish church, finally to one with a good parish church and a good pub lunch and back to the trailhead by a different route and through other hamlets.

Virtually every hamlet has its traditional parish church going back at least to the Renaissance, and a surprising number retain Norman and even Saxon features that date to the era of the Conquest. Many of them have spires or remnants of spires from later eras when each tried to outdo the others with height.[5] Others have short spires because many of the added steeples fell down— often in the middle of the night when no one was looking, village sleepers would hear a rumbling and then a crash. For retention of those ill-advised high spires, Lowth, of course, takes the prize. Most of the parish churches, despite sometimes ill advised, to the artistic mind at least, renovations to serve the twenty-first century parishioner, retain items of great beauty. After walks near Marton, Navenby, Colby and Boothby-Gaffoe, we vacated our chateau, packed our walking sticks, turned in our car, and boarded the train for London.

London itself has a plethora of historic parish churches and dozens of neighborhoods to explore, but we visit London for different reasons. We do walk there and to save money we play house, but the attractions of London are the attractions of western civilization. In London the reduced scale is of quite a different variety. London is one of the largest cities in the world with commerce, traffic, crime—a little but not violent—tacky shopping districts and flat, right-angled new high rise buildings along side the ancient and gorgeous architecture, interspersed with the classic theatres, amidst the parks and gardens. But despite the size of its population, despite the intrusion of contemporary architecture and tackiness, despite the plentitude of its arts, despite the variety of its neighborhoods and its great ethnic diversity, London is pretty small.

---

[5] Alec Clifton-Taylor, *English Parish Churches as Works of Art* (Oxford, 1989) provides wonderful information on his subject including a great deal about towers added in centuries after the church was built. He also mentions the towers tumbling, but one needs to visit individual towns to get the stories of waking in the morning to a church with no tower.

Part of the attraction of London is, of course, that it's a great world urban center, and in most urban centers, including New York, people do a lot of walking. But a major difference between New York and London is, again, one of scale. In New York, if you wish to get anywhere near the other end of Manhattan, you need to take the subway. The area in London, however, is so compact that energetic visitors can pretty much walk wherever they want to if they have the proper residence. And this time we did.

We took a "mews cottage" for two weeks with no plans except to see a lot of plays. "The Cottage"—that is its name—is a couple of centuries old and it is historic in its own unobtrusive way. It is in the mews behind the last house on Great Cumberland Place not to have been bombed in the Blitz; our address and those to its right were eighteenth-century charming, those to the left were 1960s boring and functional. To get to The Cottage one needs three keys and some stamina. One enters the eighteenth-century front door with the first and newest key, then passes through a tastefully and usefully restored hallway to a small door at the far end. Through the door we go down the winding stairs, through another hall past "The Basement," as the lower level dwelling is called. With the oldest key, we pass into the mews, a small courtyard where a lovely, large but delicate spider with a leg span of about two inches continually repairs her web.

We are told by the owners that the courtyard is her long term home. Across the courtyard, with the third key, we finally enter The Cottage. This trip would not be considered inconvenient to the average Londoner. After all, there is the three foot square elevator if one cannot possibly manage her load—we did use it to ship luggage—and the location is perfect. The Cottage is only about three blocks from the tube, the same distance from the laundromat, within a quarter mile of many fun restaurants, multiple pubs and any kind of market one could wish for, and it's less than a half hour walk to the West End. Oh, and did I mention, a couple blocks away is Hyde Park where one can rent a deck chair for a morning's read or walk along the Serpentine or just use the park as a short cut to the Victoria and Albert Museum?

A quick tube ride if you haven't time to walk the mile or so takes one to the South Bank where the Tate Modern, the London Eye (that huge Ferris wheel you see in post-millennial London brochures), the three National Theatres, the new Globe

Theatre and a breathtaking moonlight walk along the Thames where the Houses of Parliament, Big Ben, St. Paul's across the water are all crunched together. Dick used that quick tube ride the day we arrived. As soon as our train pulled into Waterloo Station after noon on Saturday, we bought *Time Out*, the weekly magazine of London doings and learned that the following day was the final day for a vast Frida Kahlo exhibit. When we arose on Sunday morning, I sent Dick on the tube—time was short—to the Tate Modern to get afternoon tickets while I waited for our house-mates, David and Mim, to join us. Dick came back with some of the last tickets to be sold for that exhibit for the final entry time. Because the Tate Modern itself is vast (nothing compact, nothing dense about that space), we spent a leisurely afternoon with the Mexican artist whose works are so rarely seen here. There were lines to gain entrance, but inside the exhibit people milled, took time to contemplate a painting, and revisited ones they had already seen for comparison.

The Cottage is tiny for all its two stories and two bed-rooms; it's a bit larger than the Chateau—the second bedroom actually has room for a desk, a chest, a single sleeper hide-a-bed and built in cupboards on all sides and still room to move about. The rest of the cottage is so filled with furniture, art and books—we rented it from friends of friends—that inhabitants are pleas-antly crowded. The four of us shared the wee space and the expense and the fun. We had to take a photo to prove that we could get into the kitchen at the same time even if we couldn't move—some readers might remember a segment of the Brit Com *Keeping Up Appearances* where Hyacinth entertains in a borrowed vacation retreat and her guests get stuck together in the narrow kitchen so that no one can move.

Scale applies to time too. In that two weeks, we managed to see twelve plays—eleven of them superb—walk the familiar streets and explore some we had not seen before, go to an un-marked art exhibit in an unmarked museum, eat at Wagamama a couple of times, visit Hyde Park several times and visit Primrose Hill—a high point for Londoners in both senses of the word—and other experiences, as, they say, too numerous to mention. And we faced the possibility of a wee flood in our wee cottage. The weather for most of our visit was, as the Brits put it, "fine." But during our two penultimate days, it rained continuously for about thirty-six hours, unusual even for rainy London. It rained enough to destroy the spider's web. But the rain had stopped that final day by the time Mim and I were up. The men, as is their wont, were still abed. I grabbed my three keys to take the garbage out and opened the Cottage Door. There up to the lip of the door step, threatening to move into the cottage furnished with a lifetime of keepsakes belonging to the owners was a courtyard filled with water.

We could see what might be a drain that might be blocked. Mim and I stewed and figured. We were fearful for the antique furniture, for the books and for the danger of missing our trains. Finally, we took the ladies' way out. We grabbed the longest fork in the kitchen; Mim shed her shoes, took the fork, waded to the drain and jabbed as far as the fork would reach. Nothing. The water stayed and the drain appeared not to be the problem. By that point we were desperate and we did a desperate thing—we awakened a man. Dick came down, took charge, eschewed our fork and put his arm up to the shoulder in the drain. He came out with yucky muck and became a "mucky pup," but the water went down, the spider rebuilt her web by noon, I got the garbage out, and we all made our train schedules. Our train travel took us toward Cornwall, that confined and confining spit of land projecting southwest into the Atlantic Ocean.

Cornwall itself is a small island of sorts, and it offers many opportunities for playing house. Bound on all sides by water, the Tamar River on its east, the sea on all other sides, it is about fifty-sixty miles long, and never more than fifteen to twenty miles wide, but that's if you had a straight road which seldom happens in England and even less on the Cornish peninsula. But then, in England, a hundred miles is a major trip. One would never plan to drive the length of England in a single day, although it's no greater distance than from Minneapolis to Indianapolis. It's just not proper—doesn't leave enough time for tea, for a pint in the pub at the end. It isn't graceful to tear across the countryside like that.

Besides, there are the tailbacks[6] and the narrow roads. For every twenty miles of limited access four lane, there are hundreds of "A Roads," guaranteed to accommodate two vehicles passing each other and "B Roads," guaranteed to accommodate a car with

---

[6] A tailback in British English is roughly akin to a traffic jam except most of the time, it lasts and extends longer.

the occasional four-to-five foot "lay-by" where you can back up and pull over for an approaching car. So, if you're going to the middle of Cornwall, 150 or so miles from London, you take a leisurely train to Exeter where you rent a car—Cornwall demands a car. That is a challenge because often filling stations and car rental agencies in the United Kingdom are tiny. One needs to be alert to spy the gasoline pump perhaps five feet off the road.

And sometimes one needs to walk a block or two from the curbside rental agency to a spot of car park where the rental cars are stored. At our rental agency, we were upgraded to a "Picasso"—it was made by either Peugeot or Citroen, but it was a Picasso—imagine driving a Jasper Johns in the states. And it was huge, almost as big as the Honda Accord we drive at home. We were fearful of driving such a car on tiny Cornish roads. Actually we ended up really enjoying the Picasso, but those first sixty Cornish miles were fraught with trepidation. On the motorways out of Exeter, the lanes were narrow, the traffic confident and ferocious. But once in Cornwall proper, we left the motorway for the small roads where the British drivers as well as the hedgerows are even closer. A typical Cornish road has one eight foot lane, two eight foot hedgerows—one on either side—and one of the aforementioned lay-bys about every eight hundred meters.

Because we left London on the 8:30 a.m. train, we could still make the sixty-mile trek from Exeter to Looe and a "Cornish Traditional Cottage" before dark. We didn't have to resort to one of those lay-bys to accommodate oncoming traffic that day. In fact, we were fortunate not to discover the one lane roads until our second day in Cornwall. But we did make it to our cottage near Pelynt where in the beautiful parish church, bell ringers still toll once each week.

Most Cornish self catering Cottages are converted antique buildings—in Britain, you don't tear down and build new; you work with the walls you have. And most, if not all of them, have a "moving in" day. The way to holiday in Cornwall is to take a cottage for a week or two. Each cottage rents either from Friday to Friday or from Saturday to Saturday; we came late that Saturday, but because it's England, our landlady had provided the makings for tea and biscuits (as our Landmark Trust caretaker had in Lincolnshire). And she, considerably younger than we were, widely traveled and very well informed, directed us to the local butcher (in England, a pig can still be aged unwrapped in the front window) and the kiosk at the end of the drive where the nearby farmer sells his wares.

When we left the next morning to find the ancient fishing village of Polporo, we stopped at the kiosk seeking the strawberries listed on his sign—fresh home grown strawberries in late October! Unfortunately, he had sold the two pints he picked that morning, but when we returned that evening, fresh strawberries were waiting beside our cottage door. Although it took some detective work to find out how many pence to leave in the honor box at his kiosk, the berries were out of this world delicious and the atmosphere of trust inspiring.

Our cottage, a refurbished seventeenth-century barn, was spacious, so much so that I startled our landlady by exclaiming when we went in. Most of our Cornwall experiences in miniature were outside the house. Besides our cottage, our surroundings included our hosts' breathtakingly restored house, their two lakes, one other cottage, the residence of the strawberry grower's sister, his farm and the omnipresent British sheep. Ownership in England is confusing because often people own the buildings but not the land under them. Although all of it appears to be part of the same land parcel, the strawberry grower owned the farm, the house of his sister, probably the driveway, and the fruit and veggie kiosk. Our hosts owned the house, the cottages and the lakes. Or maybe a Duke owned the land under all of it. Each of the lakes, mind you—aerated, stocked with fish and linked by a wee dam and a wee falls—is little larger than a standard Olympic sized swimming pool, but each is rimmed with the lush tropical vegetation[7] that is typical of Cornwall and populated by melodious birds including the rare kingfisher which neither of us saw and the pied wagtail which I did.

We did make one excursion to St. Ives which in an essay devoted to the idea of much in a tiny area must be mentioned. Artists have long been drawn to St. Ives because, they say, the light is similar to the light in the Mediterranean. The beauty of St. Ives, its challenging geography, the creative architecture that

---

[7] In "earlier centuries" according to our Cornwall guidebook, one of those British explorer botanists brought tropical plants to Cornwall. They thrived; as a result, there are palm trees and other atypical vegetation in planted gardens, particularly in the extreme south. One of the tropical plants around our lake grew close to the ground and had leaves similar to a nasturtium—except they were two feet across!

geography has for centuries demanded, must be subject for another essay, but the use of space in Barbara Hepworth's garden cannot wait. Hepworth is a world renowned sculptor. Her achievement best known to Americans is the monumental abstract sculpture in front of the United Nations Building. But for pure effect and creativity, peace and art, her own garden dwarfs anything else she has done.

Hepworth had several years of knowing she would succumb to cancer, and she used those years to create a garden that would survive her. For me, at least, the garden is one of the world's beauty spots and, unfortunately, for me it is also indescribable. It reminded me of one of those gardens ancient Chinese scholars and poets created where every angle, every view through every intentional fissure provides a different work of art for the viewer. Hepworth's sculptures and her plantings are arranged so that it seems you can walk for hours without repeating yourself, but measured in feet and inches, the garden is no larger than the average suburban lawn. And it is secret. It is surrounded, like much of the United Kingdom, by the walls of long standing buildings and there is no suggestion when you enter the Hepworth museum that it hides one of the world's great gardens. Cornwall is famous for its gardens, but for me, this one was the apex of gardens open to visitors, the apex of my trip. And because it's the most challenging to describe, I shall leave it for you to visit and return to the Looe area where our cottage was and where we spent most of our week.

Because it's nearly surrounded by the sea, Cornwall has a more moderate climate than the rest of southern England and it has several ecosystems all its own and several of what might be called sub-counties. Except for the one train trip to St. Ives, we never went more than ten miles from our cottage, usually fewer than seven. And yet, we found dozens of parish churches, hiking trails, villages and the Stick of Lostwithiel to explore. Next time, we hope to visit the Lizard and the next, Lands End. Cornwall, because it has ragged edges, has many more miles of coastline than its area would suggest and the Coastal Path follows every inch of it. You can drive to the coast and walk a few miles to a village for lunch and walk back. Or you can take one of those circle paths inland where you get to the castle, buy some ice cream from the lady in the van, and walk back on a wholly different path. You can explore villages such as Lostwithiel—where unfortunately the Church is locked—but the tearooms and the Stick are open.

The Stick of Lostwithiel is a little store with a little focus. This store is ninety-nine percent devoted to walking sticks, not those high tech adjustable rods, but walking sticks carved from many woods, designed to hide a flask, engineered with a seat on the top to open when you've had enough of walking, fashioned to complement the hautest of couture. The owner is a leather smith— the store displays a few cases and hats, but mostly he does commission work. Dick pulled out a much loved wallet from our 1996 trip that was falling apart. The manufacturer had discontinued the model (unfortunately that practice has penetrated Britain). But the leather smith at the Stick of Lostwithiel smiled at the challenge, thought he might be able to repair it overnight, and permitted us to try out dozens of sticks in the meantime.

The next day we picked up the wallet duly repaired and functional, drove the Picasso back to Exeter, took the train to London, stayed the night in the Ridgemont Private Hotel, the hotel of about eighteen rooms where we usually stay in London, and came back to our large, grand, tech mad and infatuated with the new, home nation where few hotels have fewer than a hundred "units," where traffic lanes are wide, drivers less civil and nobody had tea and biscuits waiting. But we came back to our cats and, in the words of William Faulkner, our "own small patch of native soil."

Carol Dolphin

Sunset – Hotel Villa Maya

Birds of shapes/size
        colors/varieties (too many to name)
        whistle/warble
        screech/scream
        chatter/call.

A flock of white glides low over the lake,
        heading who-knows-where.
Another cluster sits high overhead,
        gracing lacy nests in a tall bare tree.
A solitary fleet-winged traveler flutters madly
toward the horizon.

The sun has dropped.
Cicadas and frogs begin their chirping.
The day is at its end.

Go away, mosquito!
Let me enjoy this peace.

Tikal, Guatemala, 2005

A Retirement Journey

It is with a sense of trepidation versus joy and happiness that I begin this essay about my retirement journey. The decision to move to Dallas, Texas is significant in that it means I have to challenge those assumptions I hold about my own life and about the culture of a different place. The feeling of trepidation comes from the knowledge of how much I will miss my friends and the neighborhood where I lived for twenty-four years, and the feelings of joy and happiness come from being grateful for having reached this point in my life in good health and in a financial position that allows me to move.

As I made the decision to retire, I knew there had to be a plan. I wasn't an educated twenty-first century person in the Western world for nothing! The plan was to sell my condo in St. Paul, move to the west coast of Florida and perhaps do some part-time teaching as a way to establish a new network of friends. My past experiences had told me that while moving is a lot of work, the hardest part is that you miss your friends. That is one of the few things our society can't speed up—making friends. I knew I wanted to live in a city that had a decent airport so that traveling would be fairly easy and not terribly expensive. The plan seemed like a good one at the time.

But like most plans, it had to be altered for unforeseen reasons. You can put your property on the market but it doesn't always sell as quickly as you thought it would. It took almost ten months from the time it was listed to the day of closing. However, this interlude was beneficial because it gave me time to reconsider my decision to move. Many people asked why I would leave St. Paul. When I thought about leaving my friends I wanted to stay, and when I thought about the length of the winter and how difficult it would be to deal with it as I aged, I wanted to leave. When I sorted through the choice, it really came down to the fact that I didn't want to continue to live in a place that has five months of winter. I have never been one of those people who attended Winter Carnival activities with gusto and joy! I was the one saying, "Let's watch it on TV!"

The most important aspect of this interlude in terms of finding a new place to live was the fact that the hurricane season in the summer and fall of 2004 really got my attention. As I watched people evacuating their homes not once but three times, I began to reconsider the choice of Florida for my retirement home. One of the nice things about this time in life is that you can change your mind. Since I'm a single person, it wasn't necessary to convince a partner or spouse that Texas would be a better choice than Florida. In addition to the climate, one of the initial reasons for choosing Florida was that both my brother and sister have homes there. I would be near family members, which is one of those things that you think about when you reach an age when the time left is shorter than the time that has passed. The change in destination upset my sister, brother and sister-in-law more than I expected. This was understandable since for the last eight years, I had been saying that when I retired I would move to Florida.

When I internalized the message from the hurricane season, though, I realized that Florida was not the choice I wanted to make. In order to have a warmer climate and friends and family, I began to seriously consider Dallas as the place to live. It has the right climate and it has a great airport. My cousins, who are also great friends, had lived there for eighteen years. They live in Plano and I had visited them enough times to know that I could live near the downtown of Dallas much as I had done in Saint Paul and be near those activities I enjoy the most, museums and theater.

When my condo did sell, the buyer offered cash. Of course, my temptation was to get on a plane and find my new home. That would have been fun! But then reality set in when I looked at all that had to be moved and my practical side took over. I knew that I really didn't have time to go to Dallas to look for a new home and be out of the condo before closing. I had planned that closing would take six to eight weeks while the buyer was approved for a mortgage. Modify the plan one more time! I had to start focusing on *pitching and packing* after living in the same place for twenty-four years. As I said earlier, moving is work!

Since I didn't know what space I was moving into, I decided the basis for whether something went with me or was tossed would be its age and whether I really wanted to pay to move it. Perhaps it seemed like more work than I had anticipated, since I hadn't done it for twenty-four years.

The movers came and picked up my things to take them to storage and the closing went off without any problems. I had dinner that evening with one of my best friends and the next morning I got into my car (a Nissan Altima which was *fully* packed with those things I thought I might need) and I drove south on I-35 towards Plano. I had the comfort of listening to NPR stations all the way. As I listened to the accents change when I stopped for gas and food, I wondered how the next part of my journey would go.

I arrived in Plano, one of the outer ring suburbs north of Dallas, a day and a half after leaving St. Paul. When I decided that Dallas was going to be my destination and my condo closing occurred so quickly, my cousins offered me their guest room as a place to stay while I looked for a new home. They were generous not only by opening their home to me but with their time and support as I figured out all the big and small things involved with establishing oneself in a new place, e.g., banks, driver's license and new license plates.

The household I moved into is made up of two adults and their fourteen-year-old son. Their college age daughter drops in periodically as well. As a single person, I felt this was going to be a great adventure in family life and it was. One of the highlights of the six weeks I spent with them was the weekend that three more fourteen-year-olds came to stay prior to going to camp together for a week. This experience was delightful, if challenging. Video games and food provide the substance of life at this age as well as trying to get the attention of the fifteen-year-old girl who lives next door. I know there was a time in my life that was like this but it is so good to be well past it. My sympathy goes to their parents.

During this time I was working with a realtor to look at condos and townhouses in downtown Dallas and the adjacent neighborhoods of Uptown and Oaklawn. I found a lovely town home in Oaklawn that happened to be empty since the owner had been transferred. Oaklawn is about eight minutes from downtown Dallas; it is a place where people walk and there are lots of trees. There is a Whole Foods store four blocks from my home. My townhouse development is made up of twenty units. This is small enough so that I have had the chance to meet many of my neighbors—who have found it unusual for me to choose to retire here, since Dallas is not on the list of common retirement locations when one reads articles about "best places for retirees to live."

If there are any "blue" parts to Dallas, this would be one of them. One of my neighbors told me he is glad to have another Democrat in the neighborhood. That statement gives new meaning to diversity. Another neighbor corrected me when I referred to Texans as Southerners. She told me they do not consider themselves to be Southerners; they are TEXANS, a proud and spirited people. They regard themselves as a people apart. When I made the decision to move to Dallas, I knew I held many stereotypes about Texans. This was not one of them. A more pleasant surprise was to realize that the editorial page of the *Dallas Morning News* doesn't always agree with the administration in Washington and with the Republican governor. I also have realized that not all Texans speak with a heavy drawl. Is there a lot of big blonde hair and makeup? Yes. Are the Cowboys talked about ad nauseum? Yes. Television, travel and politics haven't homogenized Texans into the rest of America. Do I think I want to become a Texan? Certainly not in the stereotypical ways. My former experience of becoming a Minnesotan makes me realize that adaptation, when it occurs, does so slowly. The picture of how adaptation affects me will be clearer when more time passes.

According to a recent article in the *New York Times*, Dallas is becoming more recognized for its art and culture than in the past. As this type of recognition increases, it will modify the images of Southfork and President Kennedy's assassination that come to mind when most people think of Dallas. The famed architecture of downtown Dallas is about to be enhanced by the Trinity River Project. This is the largest public works project the city of Dallas has ever attempted. The most noticeable part of it will be two bridges designed by Spanish architect Santiago Calatrava. The first bridge will promote the whole redevelopment of the Trinity and construction on it has just begun. Ultimately, the development will use federal highway and flood control projects to transform the Trinity River into an enormous urban park that will revitalize the center of Dallas. The anticipated completion date for the entire project is 2011.

While this change is in process, there are some things that will remain the same. The twenty-four-day state fair that is the largest exposition in North America occurs every October. At the entrance, one receives a "Howdy" from Big Tex, the fair's fifty-two-foot-talking-cowboy mascot. The attraction here, like state fairs everywhere, is the fried food. During the fair, there is also the Texas-Oklahoma football game, which is something like the rivalry between the Green Bay Packers and the Minnesota Vikings. The national touring company of a Broadway show plays on the stage at Fair Park during the fair as well. This year, the selection was *Wicked*. There are a number of small theater groups here as well as a concert and speaker series offered on the campus of Southern Methodist University, which is five minutes away from my front door.

I have also had the chance to see the best of Dallas and Texas when Katrina struck in the summer of 2005 and the evacuees from New Orleans began to arrive. The city of Dallas opened its shelters. Thousands of people volunteered to help the Red Cross. Eventually all the evacuees were moved into temporary housing. There were "Spirit of Texas" campaigns to raise money for the people whose homes were destroyed in Louisiana and Mississippi. Finally, television and radio stations announced on a Monday that all the evacuees had been moved out of the shelters, but by Wednesday of the same week, there was a storm heading for Houston called Rita and the shelters re-opened to provide assistance to all the new evacuees. Many of the evacuated families stayed here. Most churches adopted groups of them and the school systems at all levels found places for the children and young adults who wanted to attend college. The teachers and administrators struggled to meet the needs of children who have no academic records. There was no question that there wouldn't be help for these families. To Texans, this is a reflection of what they mean by spirit and it is something to be greatly admired particularly since the federal government could not seem to function at any level of effectiveness.

As I mentioned earlier, winter was one of the reasons for moving south. As I sit at my computer today, the temperature is in the seventies and it's November. The climate here is much like Florida. July and August are hot, dry and rather awful. One is grateful for air conditioning. A thrill in living here is the great light. This is also one of the reasons Florida appealed to me.

In my last administrative role on campus, I had the responsibility of hiring supervisors for our student teachers. Most of the supervisors were retired teachers or principals. They always seemed to be the happiest people. I can now understand why. I remember one of them telling me he would only supervise enough students so that he still felt he was retired. I would laugh when he said that, but now I more thoroughly understand his point. I feel it is my great fortune to have a defined benefit pension, good health care coverage and the freedom to have a plan for the day or to have no plan. My goal is to keep the balance between "work" and play.

For the last two months I have been focused on unpacking and settling into my new home. I am also getting more familiar with the neighborhood and the city. For a while there, I was just making trips to Home Depot and finding people to paint, wallpaper, etc. Now I don't have to take only major roads and I haven't gotten lost lately. I have signed up to volunteer at the adult literacy program. This is something I did in Saint Paul for many years and it is one of the most satisfying experiences there can be. Dallas, like most other cities, has an increasing number of adult residents who don't know how to read. I also plan to volunteer for an arts organization. I just haven't selected which one it will be. And then, of course, there will always be volunteer opportunities connected with elections.

I have been investigating the restaurants and museums so that when friends visit this winter, I will be able to show them around with some intelligence. My favorite museum here is the Dallas Museum of Art and my favorite museum in Fort Worth is the Kimbell. Fort Worth can be reached easily by car or by the Dart light rail system. I have a new library card. The closest public library is about five blocks away and it has a pretty good fiction collection that I have been enjoying. While I was working, I was more likely to buy books rather than take the time to go to the library. Just as I did in Saint Paul, I joined the Friends of the Dallas Library.

My travel plans have begun to take shape. Next May, I will be going to the Greek islands for twelve days with my sister. I have been to the city of Athens but I have always wanted to return to see the other parts of the country I have only read about. As a single individual, I have always spent the holidays with friends or family and that is happening this year as well. I just returned from a Thanksgiving visit to friends in Los Gatos, California. I had the fun of attending Grandparents and Special Friends day at the school where their daughter is in kindergarten. Christmas will be spent with my family and friends in Florida.

After the holidays, I'm planning to look for more travel bargains. One of the benefits of being retired is that travel dates can be flexible. There are some real bargains to be found when one isn't tied to a work schedule. The Dallas-Fort Worth airport is about twenty-five minutes from my home. Love Field is about ten minutes away, making quick trips to New Mexico and Arizona quite inexpensive on Southwest Airlines. One of the reasons I decided to retire was that I wanted to be able to travel on my own before I would need help or might not be able to go at all. Since I am in good health, I don't think this will happen any time soon, but I see instances around me when the unexpected has happened. I'm realistic enough to know that something could happen to me too, but in any event, I plan to live to ninety.

I've been in Dallas long enough now that friends and family want to know how it's going and if it feels like home yet. These are normal questions. I know I'm still learning how I will adapt to the differences and nuances between Minnesota and Texas. But at this point in my life, it becomes fun rather than bothersome. I haven't been here long enough, though, that I don't miss my friends. Of course, we stay in touch by e-mail, but as everyone knows, that's not the same as seeing and talking in person. Some friends will visit this winter. I'm planning to spend a good share of summers visiting Minnesota, Wisconsin and California. This was also part of the plan when I thought I would be living in Florida. I have come to the conclusion that there is just no place to live that is perfect twelve months of the year!

In order to make new friends here, I'm planning on trying to find a part-time teaching position at either a four-year college or a community college. Any number of these is within driving distance of my house. Recently, I attended an Adjunct Faculty Recruitment Fair at one of the community colleges. Our high-tech world provides a way of having one's résumé available to the entire community college system with the click of a button. I have also been visiting local yarn shops since I will use my knitting hobby as a way to make new friends. I have been a hand knitter most of my life. It is one of those hobbies that are now having a resurgence in American life. Knitting has become trendy. I belonged to a knitting group in St. Paul and I'm hoping to form one or find a new one here. Knitting has always been a way to use my creative side and it is also a great way to relax. I'm pleased that a really good yarn shop recently opened in the neighborhood adjacent to mine. I'm sure I will become a regular there.

As I do the final editing of these thoughts, it is a sunny, bright December day here (only fifty degrees, cold by Texas standards). Minnesota and Wisconsin residents are digging out of the first big winter storm of the season. I'm glad to be here. However, my location is only one of the things that serve to make me glad. A few weeks ago, I saw an interview with Neil Armstrong on television. The interviewer was trying to get him to agree that the most important thing in his life was the fact that he was the first man to walk on the moon. Armstrong would not agree, and he pointed out that one had to look at the ledger of one's whole life to understand what is important. I feel both a sense of pleasure and joy that I have the time and resources to add to my ledger. My journey continues with gratitude to those who have helped me in the past and to those who will continue to help me find the new opportunities and challenges in this new journey in my life.

Work without Borders

Man is so made that he can only find relaxation
from one kind of labor by taking up another.

Anatole France

Leland L. Nicholls

So What to Do in Retirement?
Meet Katrina and Rita

After thirty-eight years of teaching and administration, I retired in 2004. My tenure in academe was a series of rewarding careers within a career. My experiences including a chance to travel to forty countries were challenging and enjoyable. Serving more than eight thousand students was a great honor. Now, what would fill this major void in my time to say nothing about where to direct my energy?

One new retirement opportunity centered upon the Red Cross. My wife, Mary Jean, had retired four years earlier from twenty years of teaching middle school English. She was now busy with a variety of volunteer civic services. She had already been volunteering with the Red Cross as a Disaster Action Team member with a former colleague. When her partner died, I decided to take her place. We served the victims of only one local house fire in my first year. Mary Jean was a seasoned veteran of DAT service. Neither of us, however, had volunteered or thought much about serving the Red Cross outside the local area. In late August of 2005, Hurricane Katrina changed our thinking.

We watched the news and weather reports with great interest, especially since we had purchased a second home in March in Natchez, Mississippi, some three hours up the Mississippi River from the Gulf Coast. Katrina hit the coast on Monday, August 29, 2005, with a Category Five wind force and a nearly thirty-foot high wave surge. More than ninety-thousand square miles of land took the impact of wind, water, and fire damage in Louisiana, Mississippi, and Alabama. The magnitude of the disaster was too much for us to comprehend.

So it was out of a cozy comfort zone of enjoyable retirement routine and into training to volunteer for Red Cross service in the South. We trained for disaster recovery Shelter Operations and Mass Care Management without really knowing what to expect. We agreed, however, that I, if called, would serve first, return home for a week, and then Mary Jean would go south for her three-week assignment.

After our training, I received a call from the local chapter of the Red Cross to report immediately to Hurricane Katrina disaster Relief Operation #865-06. On September, 14, 2005, I found myself en route to the Red Cross Staging Headquarters in Baton Rouge, Louisiana.

My first night's lodging was at the Our Lady of Mercy Catholic Church in Baton Rouge. After a satisfying meal and a night's sleep on a cot, I returned early the next day to the staging center (an unoccupied retail building) for orientation and field assignment.

At orientation a trainer from Alaska welcomed a new class of thirty volunteers from across the U.S. and Europe, Mexico, South America, Southeast Asia, Australia, and New Zealand. Our first handout, a Public Affairs Desk Media Release dated September 5, 2005, read:

> The American Red Cross' current priority in Louisiana is to ensure evacuees have food, water, and a safe place to stay. Once that priority is met, Red Cross will begin working with families on individual recovery plans.
>
> Given the magnitude of Hurricane Katrina, we continue to focus our resources and personnel on sheltering and feeding evacuees. As the Red Cross transitions to the next steps in the recovery process, we will keep the public informed. . . .

Another handout from the Operation's Director warned that:

> This might require that you perform duties other than those for which you were recruited. I hope your assignment is fulfilling both professionally and personally as you provide services on a disaster operation of unprecedented scale!

My mind spun with uncertainty during orientation. The

trainer continued:

Welcome to Louisiana! There are four kinds of poisonous snakes. . . . Fire ants bite at once and the shock comes two-three hours after bite. The alligators lost their homes, too. Cleanliness and hygiene are important. Keep your gas tank full. Be impartial and fair. Commonsense and courtesy are important. Zero tolerance of abusive behavior. Confidence . . . When meeting media representatives . . . Think!!! Never . . . Performance review before you leave. Confirm return travel reservations. Out-process . . . Transition back home. . . .

Additional considerations:

- Thousands of people missing or dead,
- 500,000 homes destroyed or affected,
- 1.4 million displaced people being relocated to fifty states,
- 80% of victims having never traveled outside of Louisiana,
- 40% of businesses in Louisiana damaged,
- Diverse population of tightly knit cultures,
- 50,000+ military troops activated
- Fraud warnings,
- Missing people locators,
- Mosquito control,
- Tax filing extensions for evacuees,
- Shelter services,
- Unemployment applications,
- Keeping children in school or college,
- Tuition waivers,
- Food Stamp Program,
- Rescuing or finding a pet.

So, with much on my mind, I proceeded to my first assignment.

Assignment #1
Report to Plaquemine Parish Disaster Recovery Center in the Carl Grant Civic Center as a general mass care management worker.

Four volunteers from Wisconsin and California left orientation and headed to Plaquemine, Louisiana, for the next phase of our service. The situation was a drastic change from gardening on a summer's day in Wisconsin. Here, I found four hundred evacuees occupying the entire floor of the Civic Center. My duties included everything from food service, unloading and sorting clothing and supplies, garbage detail, playing games with kids, talking, listening, and watching the shelter. All of us were still in a state of shock and bewilderment. The situation and environment seemed to be simultaneously ugly, sad, and frustrating, but we were trained to be patient, flexible, fair, etc. We were, however, also in it together, both victims of the weather in a strange place, with new neighbors living on cots less than a foot from each other.

Just as I was beginning to understand the routine of my assignment duties and new friends, we received orders to close the shelter and prepare for another move to Monroe, Louisiana. Within two days we had completed the closing procedures and started packing lunches and people for the four and one-half hour trip via school buses to northern Louisiana. Approximately one hundred evacuees and staff made the move to a new home. For some of the people this was their third or fourth relocation within the past three weeks. Our new home was to be a new experiment in disaster recovery. The new model concept was called a Community Residential Center (CRC).

Assignment #2
American Red Cross Community Residential Center (CRC), Monroe, Louisiana

Governor Elizabeth Blanco was quoted in our newsletter about the Center as follows: "We asked the Red Cross to create a community spirit in this temporary shelter with things like health care, child care, a post office, and job placement. This is the first such model, and it has been powerfully done."

The CRC was located in a recently abandoned State Farm Insurance regional office building. It seemed, in some ways, like reporting to work in corporate America. Well, not really. The CRC organizational chart was impressive and provided the foundation with a sound model for a new level of mass care management and shelter operations management. The model and operations team structure had within one building many excellent components such as local, state, and national partner services, marketing, communications, facility management, health services, community services, information management support, materials support, staff services, individual client services, evacuee and staff registration, feeding, community programs, and multiple directors. In sum, we were now in a building with a capacity, according to the Fire Marshall, of 2,300 occupants. It was a microcosm of a small town in one building, protected inside and out by most known military and law enforcement agencies. We had nineteen basic rules and reminders of getting along with each other. So, it was a "shelter" that was free to any evacuee, with free medical care, child care, counseling, clothing supplies, breakfast, lunch, and dinner, and 24/7 security. We had FEMA, Roto-Rooter, U.S. Postal Service, eye clinic, dental clinic, a pharmacy, client store, cafeteria, a fleet of emergency relief vehicles, athletic events, FBI, visiting musicians, a resident (an evacuee) barber, clergy, televisions, computers, immunization services, a large warehouse, photo ID cards, cash distribution services, airport-like security scanners, surveillance cameras, a library, nursery, playroom and toys, touch football games, transportation services, and more. In sum, it was, however, a mostly safe, air conditioned, and generally workable plan and place.

My assignment at the CRC consisted of managing Special Needs Transportation. When not on call, I had other odd jobs such as toilet checks for supplies and maintenance, supplying bottled water to a cooler near the information desk, and other general client and staff requests. There was plenty to accomplish and think about during a typical twelve-to-fifteen hour work day.

For the next sixteen days, I made more than 330 trips to Monroe area medical centers, government agencies, and other locations with clients and staff with special needs. These special needs included appointments for sick babies, kidney dialysis, lacerations, spider bites, broken bones, lab work, job drops, addiction treatment centers, airport and bus connections, employment agencies, and hospital visits. All of the requests were important, but some were more urgent than others. Regardless, my driving time with evacuees and staff during my nearly 1,500 miles of local area travel permitted me an opportunity to hear stories of their plight, miracle rescues, and to see their tears and share their hopes for a better future.

Yes, in their displacement, I saw evacuees show emotional and physical rage. There were even arrests and all the other compressed characteristics of small and large town life. In general, however, life at CRC was gradually returning to some degree of normalcy after nearly a month from the date of the storm.

Mary Jean encouraged me to keep a journal. So, I did. While I never wrote in front of the clients, I recorded their words as soon as possible so I wouldn't forget. I found their language to be beautiful, colorful, and poignant. The following dialogues may give the reader a sense of evacuees' and staff concerns in a complex situation.

Spotlight

(From "What's Happening at CRC", September 26, 2005, p.1 in the "Spotlight an in-house bulletin"):

> New Orleans resident S. came to CRC three weeks ago with her mother, three siblings, fiancée, and two children. "My mother has been getting a lot of help at CRC. I like to help other people with special needs. We all need to support each other during this time. One day, I hope for a good education for my children, a computer and car, and a meet up with Oprah!"

Rescue

(Mr. C., evacuee describing his rescue to me):

> More than fifteen of us were on the roofs of our houses. The four houses were arranged in a small square shape. My two boys were playing in the water because they were wearing life jackets and thought it was fun. I told them to get on out of the water. Just then, it was like the hand of God parted the water around the sidewalk boundaries of the houses. It was like Moses in a movie, but real. It was unbelievable how that water parted. The helicopter arrived. The first boy was hoisted up. He smiled and waved

back to us, so I knew it was safe. I was scared, but after the boy got in, I was OK with the idea of the ride up into the 'copter. I got in the 'copter and realized I didn't need my material things. I lost them all anyway. You know, I don't believe in miracles much, but I sho' have good testimony at church now. God sho' was with us!

Stars

(Anonymous comment on the stars):

After Katrina passed, it was a clear night. I have never seen such a clear night in all my life. It seemed like you could reach up and touch the stars. They were really bright! God was letting us know that he was still in charge.

Job

(Mr. W., evacuee commenting on what he would do if he got a job):

Man, I would get me a big Sonic burger, large banana shake, and double sides. Boy, that will fill you up!

(NOTE: He got the job and his wish for a big meal. The job lasted for one week but was extended to thirteen days at $12 per hour. I have never seen a person so delighted with such a short tenure.)

Relocating

(Mr. L., a street minister to Project residents):

I just had a heart operation and found myself up to my butt in water in the Project. I can't believe people was stealin' from each other. I been evacuated to Lake Charles, Shreveport, and Monroe in one week. Man, I am tired and I can't run no more!

Red Cross Shelter

(Ms. E., woman from New Orleans commenting on Red Cross shelter):

> I am sure happy to be here. There are no guns, ambulances and sirens all night. I don't know what to expect now.

T-shirt

(Text on back): "If the cook ain't fat, I ain't eatin' it."

Acts of God

(Mr. C., evacuee mulling the meaning of life after being separated from his newborn grandson by Katrina three weeks earlier):

> God done put the brakes on us. He must have some sense of humor to make me start all over at age fifty-five. But I am sure He has a plan for me. And, He ain't shortchanged me yet. I don't know where my kids are. I think one boy is in Houston. He got out with his family. I did call my boy in Baltimore and talked to my fifteen-year-old grandson. He said, "Grandpa where are you? I been waitin' to hear from you so I can come to help you." We are all blessed. Do you know anything about the Angels of Mercy? I was told by a Red Cross volunteer they might help get my grandson down here.

(NOTE: I checked into Angels of Mercy services. They could not help him.)

Rebuild New Orleans?

(Comments by a local emergency room patient to an evacuee from New Orleans):

> Mr. H. (New Orleans): What do you think about talk about rebuilding N'awlins"?
> Mr. O. (Monroe): Aw, I don't know. It's too early to tell yet.
> Mr. H.: I know what to do. They ought to bomb the place. They could call it Lake Orleans. Man, there sho' would be good fishin' in that lake.

Mr. O.: (Silence and change of subject.)

Loss

(Two sheriff's deputies eating breakfast in shelter break room after transporting prisoners to Monroe from prison in southern Louisiana to escape Hurricane Rita):

> Me: How you guys doing?
> Deputy #1: Not very good. We just got word from my wife that Rita sent a twenty-two-foot high wave through our houses and wiped out our city. Our families escaped though.
> Deputy #2: My house took twelve feet of water in 1957.
> Deputy #1: Well, I guess we had better hit the road and head back to nothing. See ya.

Cajun Philosophy

(Cajun Fisherman, heard on National Public Radio interview with eighth-generation fisherman from south Louisiana):

> We have an old saying: "You should always be nice to your neighbor, since you never know when you may have to sleep in his bed."

Cell Phone

(Nicaraguan evacuee immigrant from New Orleans):

> Evacuee Friend: Aren't you mad as hell about your cell phone being stolen?
> Mrs. G.: Lady, you must be crazy. I just lost my house and everything I own. I can only laugh about my cell phone.

Ice

(Group of well-off evacuees requesting help):

> Seventy-year-old son: Sir (to me) could you get us some ice?
> Me: How much ice do you need?
> Seventy-year-old son: It's for my dad (over ninety-years-old) here. He needs a cup of ice to put in this little cooler for his insulin.

A few minutes later:

> Me: Here you go. I hope this helps.
> Father: God bless you, son.
> Son: God bless you.
> Wife of son: God bless you. You don't know how much this means to us.

(NOTE: Unfortunately, I do know how much it means. My granddaughter and I are Type one and two diabetics, respectively.)

Funeral

(Evacuee describing his escape from Katrina and New Orleans to me):

> Part of my family went to the convention center. I took the rest of the family and drove north until the car ran out of gas. We hitched a ride to Monroe. I then got word that my eighty-four-year-old grandfather died at the Convention Center. The next thing I knew, a Red Cross worker took me to the funeral and then back to get my car. She filled the gas tank and gave me a hundred dollar bill. What a woman she was! I will never forget her!

Heat

(An incoming evacuee from escaping from Rita):

> The Red Cross had better get with it, including some water to the people on the bus that just arrived. A guy next to me died of heat stroke this morning before we left Leesville. We are tired and thirsty! Hurry, please get us some water!

(NOTE: I requested that a pallet of bottled water be delivered to the new arrivals. Later, I heard that most of the water was taken by people leaving the shelter for new destinations. The temperature hit 113 degrees in my car that day. I guess it didn't matter who got the water.)

New Money

(Ms. R., evacuee to two-year old daughter upon receiving her FEMA check):

> Girl, we got money!

Lost and Found Box

The cardboard box in the shelter was full of car and house keys. I guess it would be, since many people had lost both car and house.

New Apartment

(Evacuee's discussion with male friend on way to new apartment):

> Honey, this is great! Wow! It's near a Wal-Mart. Look at those trees. They sure are beautiful. Our new place is near a convenience store. Wow! What's that, a paper mill? Maybe that's why rent is only $64 per month. Anyway, it's still like winning the lottery!

Evacuees Helping Evacuees

(Mrs. J., age 74, commenting on her escape):

> My eighty-four-year-old husband was a resident in a nursing home. I helped the staff prepare the evacuation of a hundred residents via helicopter to a nursing home in Monroe. I don't know how we did it. God just gave me the strength to move those people. My legs and ankles were so swollen. Anyway, I got him settled in a home in Monroe. He had a heart attack and spent twelve days in the hospital. He went back to the nursing home but had a relapse. He is back in now and like a vegetable. He is taking lots of blood transfusions. He will probably not make it now. He told me yesterday to tell you thank you for bringing me out to the hospital to visit him. He said that he hopes to meet you someday.
>
> God bless you. I will get a ride back to the shelter somehow.

(NOTE: I never saw her again. Her smile, optimism, and courage were extremely rewarding and a powerful antidote to trying circumstances.)

Wrong Music

(Comments to me en route to dialysis appointment):

Mistah Lee. Man, you need some different music on yo' radio!

(I was listening to National Public Radio. Many evacuees respectfully addressed me as "Mistah Lee".)

Bro,' I am giving you an Otis Redding CD. These sounds will help you out. I gare-on-tee it.

One hour later. Another evacuee returning from his dialysis appointment:

Man, you done been jammin'! Otis Redding. Yeah! Why, he's my man! I remember when he died in that plane crash in Europe. Too young! He had horns and they sho' was wide open.

Next day, another evacuee observed while I drove him to work:

Mistah Lee. Man, what you know about that music?

(NOTE: Mr. P. was right about the Otis Redding CD being helpful. The music always got a smile and comments from my passengers. I guess it was different for them to be riding to an emergency room or doctor's office with a Caucasian from Wisconsin in a strange city—for both of us—listening to R & B from the 1960s. I never mentioned that I was a retired college professor, and they never asked me what I did.)

Dire Headlines

(The headline in The News-Star *(Monroe, LA), Friday, September, 30, 2005, p. 1 A.)*:

30% in Monroe Shelter Have Criminal Histories.

(NOTE: Later that day, my supervisor asked me if I ever felt uncomfortable with any of my passengers. Because of the pressures and pace of activities associated with the disaster relief, I had not given her question or this statistic much thought. She said that if I had any reservations about the situation to let her know and she would arrange for someone from law enforcement to ride with me. I continued my pre-headline duties. That night, while returning to the shelter with a patient on a dimly-lit rural road, I was asked if my car was a 2005, and if I owned it.

These inquiries, under the circumstances, did make me slightly nervous, but I think these feelings were generally unwarranted. Of the approximately six thousand evacuees and volunteers with whom I came in contact, 98% of them were most grateful, kind, courteous, blessed, hopeful, safe, resilient, and lucky. Their emotions were myriad in addition to being angry, stunned, isolated, afraid, hot, cold, tired, and frustrated.

So, I never thought about problem riders again. I didn't have time for thoughts like those.)

Warehouse

(My forty-year-old roommate's comments after working his first twelve-hour shift in the warehouse unloading semitrailers full of clothes, food, water, and supplies in 110 degree heat):

> Lee, as an Army veteran, I was thinking about re-enlisting. But, after today, I don't think so. In fact, I will not come to another disaster.

Feet

(A tired policeman's comments as he enters the cafeteria):

> My feet are throbbing like a sick robin's butt.

Toxic Water?

(Evacuee to me en route to hospital):

> Honey, I now got a growth between my legs after gettin' in that water.

(NOTE: I did not want to go there, so I did not comment on that revelation.)

Warning

(Evacuee comments to me after my looking askance at his friend and my next rider because we were late for her dialysis appointment):

> Hey!!! Man, I am a double schizophrenic with multiple personalities. And, man [me], you had better not piss me off. I left my family to help care for her [his friend]. Now go get that blanket to cover her during dialysis. Hurry up!!

(NOTE: I guess my questioning expression led to that explosive exchange in front of many people. It embarrassed me, but people sometimes reach their emotional edge.)

Relationship?

(Mr. P., aged fifty-five, wanted me to know that):

> I found me a new woman. But I haven't had sex with her. All she wants to talk about is the Bible and eatin'.

Escape/Rescue

(Young nurse commenting on her escape and rescue):

> The water was up to my chest and neck. I got out of the house and on to the porch but was afraid to get into the boat. It was right there in front of the door. I was still too afraid. Before I left the house, I grabbed some panties and bras, but they got wet gettin' into the boat. Had to throw them away. Sure wished I just could have saved something!

Lost Business

(Local businessman bringing displaced French Quarter musician to the shelter for a gig):

> Well, I have two cities in my sales area, New Orleans and Houston. I just lost fifty percent of my livelihood. I know

Mr. M. because he is a famous sax player near my apartment in New Orleans. He lost everything. So I have him living with me here in Monroe. I am bringing him here to play for the shelter residents today.

(NOTE: The saxophone player started to warm up for the session. I was listening to him and a food service worker walked up and said, "That music is from the heart." His saxophone music made us both tear up. It was the right music for the time.)

Hope and Prayer

(Quote from a young Sunday school student's card sent to the shelter):

I hop that you are very safe and I want you to know that I am praying for you and your family. I am glad that your family is OK. I am sad because you are pore. I love you. (Signed,) L

Spider Bite

(Evacuee's conversation with me on route to ER for treatment of Brown Recluse spider bite):

Me.: How did you escape New Orleans?
Mr. H.: Well, I was in jail.
Me.: May I ask what for?
Mr. H.: Well, I got caught smoking a joint. Yeah, just one joint. I was sentenced to thirty days in the Orleans Parrish prison, the largest in New Orleans. Must be twenty thousand prisoners in there. The building I was in had the power cut off three days before the storm hit. Katrina hit us and then our building was flooded. We were in our cells and the water was up to our necks. We finally broke out of the building but were still on the prison grounds. The prison staff decided to return and get us. They took us to another building. From there, they took us to a prison in north Louisiana. I got settled and a prisoner said, "What are you in here for? I said, "I am from New Orleans and was in for smoking one joint." He said, "Bro', this is no place for your type. This place is full of people doing twenty, fifty, or

life." After a few days, a guard came and informed me that they had found my name on a computer list of sentence records. He said that they would transfer me immediately to a Red Cross shelter in Monroe. Man, can you believe God done took my name from the bottom of a computer list and set me free?

Bingo

(Conversation about the cards on the floor of my car):

> Me.: What are those three cards on the floorboard?
> Mr. G.: Those are lottery tickets. I bought them for three dollars each with my FEMA check.
> Me.: Did you win?
> Mr. G.: Naw, I got them, but couldn't figure out how to play the game.

(NOTE: I looked at the cards and I didn't know how to play the game either. Maybe that's the point of state-sponsored gaming cards.)

Shelter Barber

(Inquiring about barber services):

> Me: Hey Bro, what's happening? Do you have a barber shop here in the city?
> Mr. J: No, I'm a resident of the shelter.
> Me: You mean you cut hair here in the shelter as a volunteer?
> Mr. J.: Yeah, I come to cut hair each day about one o'clock.
> Me: Really? Would you cut my hair?
> Mr. J: Sure, you come back about three o'clock. I'll work you in. I been really busy.

(NOTE: I returned to have my hair cut. He noted immediately that I had more hair on my eyebrows than on my head, that my eyebrows looked like Charles De Gaulle, and, furthermore, the eyebrows must come off. He proceeded to clip them off before I knew what happened. He then cut my hair and promised me that he would "shave a line on your neck that will make yo' wife proud of you." We became good friends and joked about our hair. He had none and I was down to very little and no eyebrows. I now need a haircut and sure wish he was in my city.)

Self-starter

(Member of the staff commenting on a special shelter resident):

> You would not believe that guy I met. He came here a week ago and got his FEMA and Red Cross checks. Now, in less than a week, he got an apartment, used truck, and a job. The impressive thing is that he is seventy-eight years old. He told me that he just didn't understand the younger generation and why they aren't doing the same.

I Can't Stop Working

(Story told by staff):

> I met this lady who worked at Wal-Mart in New Orleans. She came here from the LSU stadium after the storm. She called Wal-Mart and asked them if she could get a job there. Wal-Mart personnel turned her down for the job. So she asked if it would be OK for her to come in, at no salary, as a greeter. Her proposal was accepted. She claimed that she did not want to get out of the rhythm of working.

Handshake

(Asking an evacuee about my cultural skill development):

> Me: Hey W, what's up, man?
> Mr. W: Nothin'. Just waitin' for you to take me to work.
> Me: W, You know I have been taking you to work for more than a week now and we have gotten to know each other. I do have a question though. What is the key to the "Bro" hand shake? I need to have you teach me how to properly shake your hand.

(NOTE: He grinned and taught me the three phases of the hand shake. The last part is important. It involves the gentle bumping of clenched fists. I learned later from my barber in the shelter a double-bump of the fists meant you had special vibes. It is amazing the feeling and power of such a simple gesture.)

Shelter Rules

(Hand written sign on a shelter in southern Louisiana):

- No smoking, alcohol, or drugs
- No weapons, vandalism or profanity
- No bare feet in restrooms or shelter area
- No loud music
- No running in the shelter
- Do not throw balls or play catch in the shelter
- Do not leave your children unattended
- No horseplay or jumping off the stage
- Children and non-volunteers are not allowed on the stairway or in balcony
- Please respect you neighbors and this facility, including restrooms
- Lights out and TVs off at 10 P.M. until 7 A.M.
- No re-entry to the shelter after 9 A.M.
- THANK YOU

NOTICE

You must wash your hands!

A Sign from a Young Girl in the Shelter:

Thank you for the food and clothes and shoes you give us. I am thankful for the food you gave us. I want to say thanks and it is for free. And I am thankful for the food. from: A. H., to: you

Shelter Idol?

(Young girl, out of breath):

Are you coming to tonight's show? We are having a talent show at eight o'clock tonight on the stage. Will you be there? It will be fun!!!

(NOTE: It was amazing to me that the residents of our shelter had been moved twice in less than two weeks, had only the clothes on their backs, were preparing to move again the next day, and were eager to take part in a talent show to celebrate the closing of the shelter.

Before the show the audience was instructed to refrain from booing and to be respectful to the entertainers. We were a good audience. Some of the shelter adult residents, however, were cringing and commenting on the apparently suggestive dances and choices of music. Anyway, most of us enjoyed the show. The event was puzzling to me, but it did break the stress and calm us down before the pending move and next storm.)

In summary, Hurricanes Katrina and Rita resulted in the fastest and most widespread displacement of people in U.S. history. Nearly 200,000 American Red Cross-trained disaster relief workers assembled to serve. More than one billion dollars of donations immediately jammed the computer systems and offices. The disaster was said by one observer to be, "a storm that had been #3 on America's list of 'Worst Possible Things That Could Happen.'" Could it have been avoided? Let's ask the National Weather Service which sent out this alert on Sunday, August 28, 2005:

A hurricane warning is in effect for the north central gulf coast from Morgan City, Louisiana, eastward to the Alabama/Florida border, including the city of New Orleans and Lake Pontchartrain. Maximum sustained winds are near 160 mph with higher gusts. Katrina is a large hurricane. Coastal storm surge flooding of eighteen to twenty-two feet above normal tide levels, locally as high as twenty-eight feet, along with large and dangerous battering waves, can be expected near and to the east of where the center makes landfall. Some levees in the greater New Orleans could be overtopped.

There are now plenty of opinions about the answer to the question posed above. I am still not sure about the logistical possibility of doing much more than was done. In spite of rumors, negative images, myths, and unsavory activities seen on television, immediate rescue and recovery personnel were working as hard as humanly possible under the circumstances. I heard tell of one policeman who scuba-dived for people (living or dead) for thirty-six hours straight. Such service work was not unusual and caused me to reflect upon the evacuees' faith.

While the inclination to say, "Why me, God?" would have been understandable, I found that the attitude of most folks I met seemed to be that God was teaching them through adversity. I didn't hear many evacuees complain that He had forsaken them. They remained steadfast in their faith. They were always talking about Him.

There was also a sense of cohesiveness, color blindness, sharing, and dignity among shelter residents. I saw many evacuees looking proud and good. It was important for them to look good despite their troubles.

My Hurricane Katrina experience taught me to appreciate the work of large and small church congregations and civic and grassroots' organizations pitching in to help and give where and when needed. The Red Cross volunteers demonstrated a new meaning of teamwork for me. Yes, my values toward materialism changed. Class, race, and neighborhood loyalty are very complex. I made new friends. I now have more empathy for the suffering masses and the work of those people who serve. Patience *IS* virtue. Saying good-bye to someone displaced with no possessions and no forwarding address was really difficult for me. The hurricanes showed us the wide difference between the power of surviving and power of thriving. The most powerful lesson of the experience, however, is about gratitude, first for the support of my wife and family, and second for the thankfulness of evacuees, friends, and acquaintances.

My educational career centered upon the subjects of the social sciences (geography, history, sociology and civics), plus hospitality and tourism, and later, service management. The aftermath of Katrina and Rita led to my laser-like focus upon these disciplines and more. To participate in and view the complexities and interactions needed for the initial hurricane relief and recovery efforts, the raison d'etre for my education became apparent. Not, however, at the expense of so many people. The events were the ultimate opportunity to serve fellow man in need and implement the curriculum of life.

The destruction and chaos of these hurricanes also resulted in an institutional and personal "group think." Under the circumstances, I am really not sure what could have been done any better; faster, yes. But bureaucratic organizations are usually by nature slow to respond. Some weak links of service will likely be researched and improved upon next time. For example, residents of prisons, nursing homes, hospitals and other special care facilities really do need viable disaster evacuation plans. Categorizing and defining evacuees, refugees, looters, and finders also need improvement, so that the "Blacks are 'refugees' and 'looters,' Whites are 'evacuees' and 'finders'" is not repeated.

Disaster rescue, relief, and recovery are always works in progress. They will never be perfect on the scale of this hurricane disaster. The personal and collective finger pointing and "Monday Morning Quarterbacking" seem to serve primarily as stress reducing valves. Again, governmental and service organizations were well-meaning and generally sincere in their convictions and efforts. Few groups or people on either side of the disasters had experienced a challenge of this magnitude. Eighty percent of the Red Cross volunteers were serving at their first national disaster. Only a few residents of the area had experienced the 1927 flood, 1957 Hurricane Betsy or 1969 Hurricane Camille. The country will move on, but will we bring the victims with us?

Mary Jean served three weeks in Baton Rouge and Baker, Louisiana, as a shelter manager, and although our jobs were very different, we realize that each contributed to the understanding of the other; it is good to have this experience in common. The Red Cross will continue to be a part of our retirement, and we understand that if catastrophe comes to our part of the country, help will come from all over. Katrina and Rita had much to teach us: it is never too late to keep learning, even in retirement.

Liina Keerdoja

Water Ministry

My church has an outreach program aptly called the Water Ministry, because it provides shower and laundry facilities for the homeless. And as part of the bargain, it also serves them lunch. Ever since it got started in 1989 I had been intrigued by the very concept of such a ministry and interested in how it is actually put into practice. When I retired in 2004 I was finally able to go and see for myself, and ever since, I have been one of about twenty-five active members of the Water Ministry at St. Columba's Episcopal Church in Washington, D.C.

Between September and mid-June, when the Water Ministry is in operation, I spend several hours a week among the homeless. I am part of the "also serves them lunch" crew. Most of the time I help the cook for the day (the person charged with deciding the menu and putting the meal together), and roughly twice a month I take on that function myself. Typically there are two to four people working in the kitchen. The Water Ministry is open Monday through Friday, with the exception of Wednesday. I work on Mondays and Fridays. Currently we have between twenty-five and forty-five guests each day, the actual number of regulars being somewhat higher, since not everyone comes every time.

It takes a lot of effort to operate the Water Ministry. Volunteers work with running the showers, helping with the laundry, and preparing and serving lunch. We all join forces for the annual Water Ministry Christmas party. Now and then a Sunday school class will lend a hand by baking cookies, putting together take-away snack and toiletries bags, and perhaps even preparing part of a meal. On most days, but especially when we are short of volunteers, our guests pitch in to help set the tables and clean up

147

afterwards. Clearly the Water Ministry contributes towards filling a void, since homeless shelters as a rule do not provide laundry or shower facilities nor do they serve meals.

The Water Ministry seeks neither to reform its guests nor to ask why they are homeless. There are other organizations to deal with that. Our guests have only to agree to adhere to established standards of behavior—they are requested to sign a printed form the first time they come—and in return, we are happy to welcome them. Volunteers are encouraged to chat with the guests, and whenever possible, to sit down and join them for lunch.

I know I am working for a good and worthy cause, making a small but essential contribution to society. After all, what would Washington (or any city) be like were it not for volunteer organizations that are geared to helping those on the margins of society?

But to be honest, my being part of the Water Ministry is really all about me. At any rate, it is more about me than anything else. When I first became a volunteer, I could not envision how much personal satisfaction and fulfillment working at the Water Ministry would bring me. In a nutshell, in addition to letting me see the world around me from a wider angle, being part of the Water Ministry lets me feel good about myself. Especially on days when I have been cook for the day, I go home feeling I have done something that truly matters.

Admittedly, spending a few a hours twice a week with the homeless has not given me profound insights into the problems and causes of homelessness, but it has made me see homeless people in a different light. Being among them a few hours a week, I no longer consider them outside my realm of existence. They are my fellow human beings, many of them clever and witty and more knowledgeable in certain areas than I am. And needless to say, they all have more street-smarts than I do.

Talking with our homeless guests and watching them interact among themselves has allowed me to observe how pleased people are if you remember their name, how fragile someone's ego can be and how volatile behavior can become. I see that talented and well-educated people can also be homeless. I will never forget the time one of our guests, a young man probably in his twenties, sat down at the piano in the back of the room and started to play Bach's *Two-Part Inventions.* I see also how little it takes to make someone happy. Another young man is a case in point. His face is beaming; he is happy all over for having found a needed pair of good and attractive shoes at our church's used clothes give-away. And then I think of myself coming home with a brand new pair of store bought shoes, disappointed that I did not find the exact color I had in mind. It is a humbling and a mind-broadening experience.

When I first started working at the Water Ministry, I felt certain I would never ever have what it takes to be cook for the day. Besides, I was quite happy to work with the more seasoned cooks and simply do what I was told. But as things tend to happen, after working in the kitchen for about two months, I was asked to step in at the last minute and prepare a meal all by myself for, at that time, twenty to twenty-five expected Water Ministry guests. I made chili, hot dogs, salad, and brownies, and managed to survive this sink-or-swim experience. And so, despite my initial apprehensions, quite early in the game I unexpectedly found myself designated a bona-fide Water Ministry cook. The Water Ministry has gained a reputation for serving tasty and wholesome home cooked style meals, and I am doing my best to uphold the standard.

Preparatory to being cook for the day, I spend a substantial amount of time choosing the menu and buying the necessary food. Basic staples (coffee, milk, sugar, salt, etc.) are stocked by the Water Ministry, but obtaining food items specific to the menu is the cook's responsibility. I not only have to come up with a nutritious meal (I tend to stick to casserole dishes and meatloaf), but I need also to provide an alternate choice for guests with eating restrictions—a few of our guests don't eat meat, one person is allergic to mushrooms. Then there are guests who cannot eat milk products, though there is one such guest who will throw caution to the winds when it comes to the macaroni and cheese prepared by one of the other cooks.

Since I am spending the church's money, for the first time in my life I find myself assiduously comparing food prices and checking for bargains at neighborhood grocery stores. To a large degree my choice of menu will depend on what happens to be on sale. It is a challenge of sorts to find recipes for large groups and to adjust existing ones to feed more people. An additional challenge is determining the amount of food to prepare, since we never know in advance the exact number of guests that will show up on any given day. I am encouraged by my successes and try not to feel discouraged when things don't turn out as expected. I have learned a lot, and am still learning. I have become more aware of kitchen safety and sanitation issues, an awareness I have carried over into my own kitchen. And what's more, I find that cooking for a dinner party at home is a piece of cake, now that the Water Ministry has gotten me used to cooking for larger numbers.

When I retired I not only left my job, I also left behind a network of friends and colleagues with whom I regularly shared lunches and coffee breaks. It was good to have kindred souls to talk to about mutual interests and concerns. Happily, the Water Ministry has provided me with a similar kind of social network. I have gotten to know many of my fellow volunteers quite well, and I look forward to seeing them and talking with them as we work together at the Water Ministry, giving and receiving more in return.

Judy, When She Retires Will—

You ask about retirement and how I approached it? Remember, you asked specifically about retirement. So I'll just skip all the great students, and the wonderful classroom experiences, in the interest of focusing strictly on thoughts of *retirement*.

Well, let me see—

I remember vividly

the time—

4:30 p.m., end of the semester December 1981 (I was all of forty-four years old),

the place—

My office (actually, in another life it had been a storage closet but, to give it its due, it did have a comfy womb-like feel to it)—I needed to turn on the lights to see much of anything by 2:00 on a cloudy day, which this was, and it was cold outside. As the office door opened directly on the hallway (a very efficient wind tunnel) with east- and north-facing doors opened to the outside less than fifty feet away, my wooly black pantsuit proved up to holding back winter to some extent.

and the occasion—

I had just finished another round of paper-grading conferences, just finished telling the last student that if he/she wanted to earn more than a C- on the essay, he/she could rewrite it with my comments in mind. Student's reaction to this news? "I've already got a job and I can tell you, I'll be able to buy and sell you in six months." Without missing a beat, says I, "Point taken, but if you want more than a C-, you're going to need to rewrite this piece."

And I think to myself, "For cryin' out loud—pick a subject worth both our time!" Said student "harrumphs" and galumphs out of the office, muttering under his/her breath. I hear foot stomps all the way down the hallway and the east-side door slam, followed by a whoosh of cold air.

—when the urge to retire hit me.

I definitely was not looking forward to second semester.

Fast-forward several years

(I'm now in my fifties.) Here I sit, in the cold attic of an old house that serves as the English Department office space, looking forward to January when my other "job" (as creative producer and director of a local theatrical experiment in presenting local history) would overlap with my teaching job and thinking "why don't they just let me go" and "I could quit. . . ." After all, it wasn't as if I had a tenure-track job. I was an adjunct. Would always be an adjunct. And the stomping footsteps out of the office at my suggestion that the grade could rise if several changes were made on the essay—galumphing down four flights of wooden stairs now—"Mustn't grumble," think I.

I was an adjunct. Would always be an adjunct.
I definitely was not looking forward to second semester.

Fast forward to a mid-spring semester

(I turn sixty.) Still in the English Department's attic office but now also sharing an office with three other people in the Education Department. Too early for me to consider retirement? I'm still teaching and editing my husband's trade books (very enjoyable), but and that "other" job has morphed into a fully satisfying equivalent of a full-time job—running three theatre companies and, most enjoyable of all, guiding the artistic vision of one of them.

I was an adjunct. Would always be an adjunct.

What better time to make the move!

Of course, all the fears that attend making that decision descended on me every time I seriously considered the idea. Will I really have enough meaningful work to fill my days? What if the state pension system goes broke? Would I ever need to survive on the pittance that my social security would amount to? Would I be financially compensated for what I do? Have my husband and I really covered our money bases for our retirement so that I can afford to quit working while he toils on? My *Little Engine That Could* crunches numbers and says, "I think we can." I burn my bridges.

Would never be an adjunct again.

My life in the theatre begins

Husband hurries off to his first day of school while I sit staring at the computer, looking at a script I have just rewritten for the umpteenth time. I'm having difficulty finding a voice for one historical figure from my community's rich past, but do I regret my move? Not on your life! With no business experience, I now serve as Executive Director for the management group and as Artistic Director for my theatre, Illinois Voices, one of the three theater companies that make up the Illinois Theatre Consortium. My life since retirement has revolved around this consortium that I co-founded back in '92 and I'm learning how to be an effective businesswoman.

But I must regress

Before I began teaching, I was young and mad about going into the theatre. Luckily I was pragmatic. I knew that I probably was not going to make a living acting, so I went to a school that offered me both theatre training and teacher training, my fall-back position. I acted plenty during the years between college graduation and 1981 (the time this tale begins), but clearly I wasn't about to support myself with my passion. So I went back to school to get my master's in English. Wanted to teach in junior college. Turns out the four-year university that gave me my degree also gave me an adjunct position.

However, in the early 1980's, after spending an academic year in London and seeing how any piece of written material could be turned into theatre, I began incorporating archival materials into performance pieces. I began weaving West-Central Illinois oral histories, music, and poetry into a narrative, formed a three-person touring group, and organized tours to nursing homes, historical societies, libraries, women's clubs, service organizations, and church groups that toured in Iowa and Illinois over a period of over ten years. Our merry little band was very big in the nursing home circuit where the residents seemed to delight in the doggerel written by amateur poets, sang along with the familiar melodies and even some they'd never heard before, and closely examined our costumes—including my high-button shoes.

In 1989 my husband took a job in central Illinois. To a community with two nationally recognized universities. To a community with easy highway access to the entire state. To a community with international business operations. To a community that seemed about to abandon its historical heritage. What an opportunity for me. I decided to make two immediate connections: the local historical society with its rich newspaper archive going back to the early settlement days, and Kelly Services, which would offer all sorts of openings for networking. I was about to Color my Parachute. It worked.

I began offering my theatrical services presenting programs in local history to the historical society, the library, and any organization that was interested. The commissions started coming in.

Then, in 1992-93 the Talking Books for the Heart of Illinois Talking Book Center commissioned me to develop a unique program that won an Illinois Secretary of State grant to produce a series of audiotape interviews with clients of the Talking Book Center. The result was a ten-hour, nine-tape compilation of memories collected from East Central Illinois senior citizens and Talking Book patrons. While I still could not fully support myself with theatre, I found that the passion to educate had expanded my classroom beyond four classes of twenty each, and the pay proved adequate to my needs.

Illinois Voices Theatre is my creative outlet these days, primarily through on-going collaboration with the local museum of history and a historic cemetery (we are, after all, in Lincoln Land). Together we have produced a state- and national award-winning event, actually staged in the cemetery in all weathers that "began as an effort to foster respect for cemeteries and to decrease incidents of vandalism." Since then it has evolved into a corner-stone of community history education through theatrical presenta-tion (as opposed to the kind of first-person interpretation at Plymouth Colony or Williamsburg or New Salem).

Over the past eleven years we three partners have pre-sented the human stories of many of the citizens who founded this region—the famous (does Adlai Stevenson I, Vice-president of the U.S. under Grover Cleveland qualify, or his grandson Adlai II, two-time Democratic Presidential nominee and U.S. representative to the United Nations?), the infamous (the poor woman, niece to a protestant missionary in Mexico, who threw carbolic acid on parishioners after church), the ordinary (the hundreds of immigrants fleeing oppression or famine in their native countries—Prussia, Ireland, Hungary), the good (hun-dreds of young men white and black alike who fought for this country from the Revolutionary War on), the bad (Baseball Hall-of-Famer Hoss Radbourn whose temper and bad manners were almost as legendary as his pitching arm), and the ugly (the unfortunate young jail keeper who was murdered by one of the criminals under his care, which resulted in a mob hanging). They all came through McLean County and if they died here, they were buried here and we tell their stories.

Or rather *they* tell their own stories, as much as possible through their own words, as the audience walks with a guide from burial site to burial site in this beautiful rural cemetery, listening as each actor relives a part of his or her life. At times the story is revealed from "beyond the grave" with full knowledge of a life lived to its end. Other stories are frozen at one incident in time, the person not knowing what life has in store for him or her, their families, or the world. A fictional character searching and finding the gravesite of the infant who was Frank Baum's inspiration for Dorothy Gale of Kansas told one unique story. In this particular case, Dorothy Gale regaled Dorothy Gage, Baum's niece (who died at nine months), with stories of the remarkable adventures they had in Oz. Through this annual event, the history of the county becomes real and ongoing to thousands of visitors.

If there was ever a project that took on a life of its own, *Voices from the Past: A Discovery Walk Through Evergreen Cemetery* is it. When the program began in 1995, no one had any idea that it would still be going strong eleven years later, with current planning going into 2008. No one predicted that our audiences would number in excess of 3,500 people from all over the U.S. over an eight-day period, or that we would become the gold standard for Illinois cemetery walks.

What is it that distinguishes this type of cemetery walk from countless others throughout the United States? Partnership and professionalism—of the theatrical component (trained actors, writers, director, costumer, and technical staff paid for their participation), of the museum's education and volunteer departments' dedication of resources, financial underwriting and staff time in addition to thousands of volunteer hours annually for research, guiding, and office support), and of the cemetery staff, which cooperates fully and completely for the first two weeks in October of every year, while maintaining the quiet dignity of this beautiful place during funerals that take place while the tours continue. The two weekends of the event are open to the public while several thousand school children attend during the first four days of the week in between weekends.

Not only that—this program has also expanded into teaching others, through workshops and individual contracts, how to tell the stories of their communities and organizations. Illinois Voices Theatre receives commissions on a regular basis these days to tell one or another story about Illinois' rich history. And, oh, yes, I do tour my one-woman show, *Madame Senator: A Dramatic Portrait of Florence Fifer Bohrer* (in case you've never heard of her, in 1924 she was the first woman elected to the Illinois State Senate—Ol' Private Joe Fifer's girl. Who was *he*? Why governor of Illinois before the turn of the century. Politics, it would seem, was genetic in McLean County.).

I'm available for bookings.

So, Judy When She Retires Will Do What?

"Fiddle dee dee," like Scarlett I say,
"After all, tomorrow is another day."

Margaret T. Gordon

Flexing My Spirit Again

Ten years is a really long time.
Now it's their turn
To create the vision,
Revise the mission,
Build community,
Raise the money.

It's their turn
To pace, sleepless,
Over the new budget
And planned cuts—are they
Across the board or vertical?
And to fight the battles
Over every new hire.

I have a new name—Emeritus,
And the traditional rocking chair
To go with it. There is also
A small fourth floor office,
Shared with two other ex-deans,
E-mail, free parking, a mailbox,
And a fellowship in my name.
Thank you!

No committees! No faculty meetings!
That over-tired, jaded feeling is almost gone.

Back in the building, or at gatherings,
I find myself listening but resisting
Being drawn in by the arguments,

The opportunities, the discontent.
When asked, I quietly counsel tolerance,
Understanding, and creative tension—
To save that special, vital energy
Needed for professing and publishing.

It's still comfortable for me there,
And I feel genuine gratitude
That the rules let me teach
Part-time five years, no more.
This is my second, and the stats predict
I won't opt for a third. Why?
Will I be ready then to sever ties fully?
I find I give more to students now than before,
And I know it's because there is more left.

For now I have the time I longed for.
I can focus on postponed writing, or not.
I can also read—not just skim—
Newspapers and books, even novels.
I find my thoughts turn more often to family,
Home, arthritis, exercise and health.

I am calm inside again, free to be,
To create and step up to new vistas,
Find new niches—photography,
Jewelry making, volunteerism,
Even golf, maybe bridge.
I take advantage of "senior" rates,
Afternoon symphonies and movies,
And dabbling in art walks,
Vacations during the term.

I enjoy the calm, the inner peace
Flexing my spirit and soul again.
My freedom is evolving,
Re-energizing my mind and heart.
Best of all, it lets me see that
The new ride
Will be as great as the last.

December, 2005

Women Academics,
Women's Roles

There will be little rubs and disappointments everywhere, and we are all apt to expect too much; but then, if one scheme of happiness fails, human nature turns to another; if the first calculation is wrong, we make a second better: we find comfort somewhere.

Jane Austen, *Mansfield Park*

Carolyn Wedin

Walls and Candles—
or When Will We Ever Learn?
Riffs on Retirement of a Role Juggler

Greek poet C. P. Cavafy (1863-1933) writes in "Walls":

> With no consideration, no pity, no shame,
> They have built walls around me, thick and high.
> And now I sit here feeling hopeless.
> I can't think of anything else: this fate gnaws my
> mind—
> Because I had so much to do outside.
> When they were building the walls, how could I not have
> noticed!
> But I never heard the builders, not a sound.
> Imperceptibly they have closed me off from the outside
> world.

Yes, there are definitely walls to recall, many walls, in a lifetime of balancing the roles of academic, wife, parent, home-maker, grandparent. Some of the walls have been dismantled, some crumbled, some re-erected in new, even less transparent shapes and forms. There are walls, too, in retiring from the first of those roles, the academic. Some are walls of aging, some of image, some of self-image. All walls, at all times, have been and are impacted by being from birth onward a female, a girl, a woman.

But encompassing past, present, future, another Cavafy poem reverberates as well. Between, among, even atop those walls are a multitude of "Candles":

160

Days to come stand in front of us
Like a row of lighted candles—
Golden, warm, and vivid candles.

Days gone by fall behind us,
A gloomy line of snuffed-out candles;
The nearest are smoking still,
Cold, melted, and bent.

I don't want to look at them: their shape saddens me,
And it saddens me to remember their original light.
I look ahead at my lighted candles.

I don't want to turn for fear of seeing, terrified,
How quickly that dark line gets longer,
How quickly the snuffed-out candles proliferate.[8]

"I look ahead at my lighted candles." Muckraking author
Ray Stannard Baker (who grew up twenty five miles from where I
sit at my north-woods computer, above the tumbling creek, under
the towering pines and soaring eagles), in the voice of his alter
ego, David Grayson, wrote late in life that "a man's thoughts, his
ripe experience, the treasures of his knowledge, what he has
gained in all his years of wisdom, or of beauty or of friendship
perish with him unless he has communicated them, in one way or
another, before he dies."[9] How much more is that the case for the
woman with children, whose first-person reflections are sadly
lacking in literature, corresponding with her lack of time for
reflection.

And so I attempt to look back and forward, at myself at all
my ages, including the present one, at experience which might be
of use to someone else if it can only be conveyed. Physicists tell us
there is a reason time goes faster and faster as we age, a reason for
the increasing speed with which the line of snuffed-out candles
grows. As the internal clock ticks more slowly, external time
moves more rapidly. And when I look at that short, disappearing

---

[8] *Collected Poems*, Revised Edition, Translated by Edmund Keeley and
Philip Sherrard, Edited by George Savidis (Princeton University Press,
1992), pp. 3, 9.
[9] (*Under My Elm: Country Discoveries and Reflections* (New York:
Doubleday, Doran, 1942).

time to share what I have in both pain and pleasure learned, I sense its essence is in the combination of roles, not in any single one. Through thirty-five years as an academic, as a teacher, a writer, I frequently felt that home life and my then young children saved me from many a disappointment, defeat, and despair. And now in retirement, I often feel my love of learning, and love of literature, and love of writing hold back the walls of uselessness, pointless-ness, and dread.

In "Walls" Cavafy says "I sit here feeling hopeless," and the burnt "Candles" the speaker looks back on are "gloomy," "cold," "bent." This mood I don't share, perhaps because I don't dare, but I think more because I see so much positive coming from the juggling struggle. In this attempt to write what I have learned, instead of depending only on candles, I will also look to the brilliant sunlight of Cavafy's "I've Brought to Art":

> I sit in a mood of reverie.
> I brought to Art desires and sensations:
> things half-glimpsed,
> faces or lines, certain indistinct memories
> of unfulfilled love affairs. Let me submit to Art:
> Art knows how to shape forms of Beauty,
> Almost imperceptibly completing life,
> Blending impressions, blending day with day.

(p. 116)

Many things have changed for a woman who through no particular skill in planning nevertheless ends up having it all. In my favorite fantasy film, the 1987 *Baby Boom*,[10] the Diane Keaton character, J. C. Wyatt, is a high-powered, soon-to-be-partner New York City executive who unexpectedly inherits a baby (a toddler, actually, and a toddler who gets no older as the seasons pass, but it is fantasy after all). As she struggles to combine her old and new roles, losing her male partner in the process, she is told authorita-tively and tellingly by her male boss: "You can't have it all–not you, not me, not anybody!"

As a precursor of the current "opt out revolution" (the phrase is the New York *Times*'; the research Sylvia Ann Hewlett's and Carolyn Buck Luce's, as reported in their article "On Ramps

---

[10] Directed by Charles Shyer; Written by Shyer and Nancy Meyers.

and Off Ramps: Keeping Talented Women on the Road to Success" in the *Harvard Business Review*, March, 2005) our fictitious J.C. leaves the high pressure Manhattan business world for a homestead in Vermont. In her snow-bound kitchen she has to do something, so she makes and then markets baby food applesauce, building a wholesome empire which ultimately has the big men in New York City drooling over her bottom line and eating out of her hand. Of course the multi-million-dollar success of the film ending was fancy then; fancy now. And of course the perfect combination of child sustenance and money-making entrepreneurship is a dream beyond reach, but good goals—like "having it all"—can nevertheless give us good pushes.

But "no one wants to be superwoman any more," writes Madeline Bunting in *The Guardian* about the Hewlett/Luce study of 2443 women ages twenty-eight to fifty-five from 2004. The women flooding onto the off ramp in this study, going home mostly to care for children or elderly parents, "have struggled to reconcile their femininity with a male working culture built around single-mindedness, competitiveness and self-projection," Bunting continues. And to the clichéd public reaction to such women, "if she can't stand the heat she should get out of the kitchen," Bunting sensibly suggests "it's about time we redesigned the kitchen with an extractor fan."[11] A good friend back at my own university of thirty-plus years tells me that there, too, the juggling woman seems to have left the circus, leaving in her place childless, complaining women living alone, with cleaning help.

And, truth be told, very few want to be superman any more, either, at least if it means eliminating the rest of life to succeed in business. The Fall, 2005 issue of *Macalester Today* alumni magazine has an article by Kara McGuire called "Balancing Acts," subtitled "Young Macalester parents are wrestling with age-old questions of balancing work, life and child rearing." Questions and challenges haven't changed much, but here and elsewhere, there is definitely more bi-gender participation in the struggle—a few men staying home, more sharing of child-care and household duties, so perhaps my little flashlight beams into my past could be of interest to young men of today, too.

---

[11] I am grateful to my daughter, Monika Byrd, Director of Leadership Development Programs, Phi Theta Kappa Honor Society, Jackson, Mississippi, for suggesting I look at the Hewlett/Luce study.

I must begin by noting, reminding us all that much out-right discrimination has been eliminated for the woman who hopes or dares or tries to "have it all"—children, maybe a husband or partner, rewarding career. No longer, I hope, will a young woman high school senior wanting to be a doctor be told by a counselor that she should be a nurse, since it fits well with inevitable marriage and parenting, but since her math and science grades are so high, she should definitely aim for "head nurse." (Bunting, however, refers to psychologist Anna Fels' current book, *Necessary Dreams*, suggesting that ambition is carefully and thoroughly extracted from young girls still today).

No longer will a female recipient of a prestigious graduate fellowship receive less money than a male holder of the same award if they are both married, as was the case with the Woodrow Wilson Fellowship (I guess the name says it all?) I was awarded in 1961. Hard to believe now, but a man also got an even larger stipend when he had children; not so if the one who carried the child also carried the fellowship. Is it progress when things have been evened out so that neither the male nor the female scholar gets extra money for marriage and children?

I hope there may be, but do not know of, research which demonstrates that some less blatant things have changed too—for example, the grades of women and men. Saul. D. Feldman, in his 1973 book, *Escape from the Doll's House: Women in Graduate and Professional School Education,* documented the unsurprising reality that in those days when men graduate students married, their grades went up; when women did so, their grades went down, and, yes, when men divorced, their grades went down and when women freed themselves of those surly bonds, their grades went up. Since the Macalester article indicates that cooking, cleaning, washing are today more gender equal for academic couples, let us hope that those grade disparities have evened out, too. I do think it likely, though, that young women and young men juggling roles today feel frequently just like I often did and do—that what one really needs is a good old-fashioned wife.

Feldman did not have a category for married women with children, but if he had, I doubt not that my own case would have been typical for the 1960s and 1970s—the only "C" I have on my academic record, undergraduate or graduate, was the spring of 1963—and even that was unjustified. A professor at the University of Kansas had graciously allowed me to take an incomplete in his seminar, pending my final paper and the birth of my first child in April, but I had, unfortunately, the unwitting audacity to turn the paper in that summer on the day he was leaving for Europe. Five minutes later it was returned to me unmarked except for a large red letter on the front that I quickly determined did not stand for "Carolyn."

Job hunting and demands, too, have changed over the years, at least on the outside. Surely no department chair would dare put into writing what I have in a letter of 1965 from a Wisconsin college: "You have an outstanding record, but I see that you have two small children and I wonder how you can hope to do the demanding job in our department and also care properly for them." (Even in those unenlightened days, I remember thinking: "Wouldn't my outstanding record AND two small children tell this guy that I am Super Woman and he should grab me fast?")

It is to be hoped that more search committees at ever higher levels have significant numbers of women members with role-juggling experience. On a University of Wisconsin-System Search Committee for Vice President of Academic Affairs in the late 1970s, it was almost humorous when one of the male members (a Dean of Letters and Sciences from one of the UW-System campuses) made a huge deal of "an unexplained gap" of several years in a female candidate's credentials. We three women on the committee looked at each other simultaneously. We, and only we, had noticed that the years he was suspicious of coincided with the birth dates of her children.

I can only hope, since I don't know, that male professors have stopped leaving meetings at 5:30, "because my wife will have dinner waiting" while the female who has a comparable dinner to fix when she gets home is still there. (Perhaps it still happens, but they don't say anything?) Maybe young fathers are no longer fawned over for their occasional child care while the young mother's constant care goes as unnoticed as wallpaper? And certainly health plans everywhere have corrected the oversight which, when my third child was born, meant that an employee could be covered for a DWI auto accident but not the birth of a child? (I am proud to say that at least in part, due to the fact that many of us UW-Whitewater professors had in those heady anti-war days joined the Teamsters' Union, I and my son Brendan became the first University of Wisconsin System beneficiaries of the corrected, more inclusive policy, made retroactive by the Board of Regents to cover his birth date.)

Over all those years, not all of the bias came from men or rules and regulations, of course. Women who *had* believed that they could not have it all and had given up husband or children for their academic careers had no admiration or empathy for the weary woman wayfarer on the road less traveled, as with the head of a summer Upward Bound Program in Illinois who, I am convinced, failed to hire my husband and me despite our extensive experience with Upward Bound in North Carolina because I was then nursing Brendan.

Whether this has changed, I cannot judge, but these decades later, I see in the New York *Times* that a passing remark by Barbara Walters that she was made uncomfortable by a woman nursing next to her on a plane has led to a protest by "lactivists" in front of ABC headquarters and that at least six states have passed bills saying a woman is entitled to breastfeed wherever she "is otherwise authorized to be."[12] Where was this militant nursing when I needed it? Not only could it have prevented a lot of tedious expression of milk into tiny bottles, but it could have kept the front of my blouses dry in front of freshlings who got younger every year and could literally bring my milk down with their childish exclamations.

So are you embarrassed yet? Because I am leading to what should be obvious—that much has changed, but so much more hasn't changed a whit, and the remainder has only changed masks. All those struggles, all that learning, all the successes in keeping all those little balls in the air—"A gloomy line of snuffed out candles"? Couldn't it somehow be otherwise? Couldn't my candles of the past be "golden, warm, and vivid," giving some light to some other young woman's present and future? Aren't there things that would help all those young mothers flocking around this year's "problem without a name"? Judith Warner writes in *Perfect Madness*—"you want to be perfect and you want to have everything"—but what we expected as single childless women and what we have encountered after acquiring a family, she adds, is like a kind of wall. Or it could be as Ellen Goodman suggests: "'Many women today,' says Harvard Business School's Rosabeth Moss Kanter, 'want to be both their mother and their

---

[12] "New York Report," June 7, 2005, A19.

father.' Even if mom never color-coded napkins and dad never made the Fortune 500, Martha [Stewart] has become a high-profile variation on the theme of having it all if you can do it all."[13] Couldn't my experience help someone somewhere going through the same thing, inventing all those wheels all over again and again and again?

For looking back now from the grand perspective of having bungled through the juggling jungle what I really do see are still glowing candles that continue to light my way in retirement. My essential philosophy of life is serendipity, happy accident, for I see no way I could have planned and executed such luck as to have three beautiful grown children whom I like and a job which, except for the paper grading, was so full of variety, fresh starts twice a year, interaction with interesting people, encouragement of writing.

Yet academic work and life may lend itself to role-juggling better than many or most careers, at least in days gone by. Flexibility of schedule meant I could get up at 4 a.m. to finish marking the papers foiled by early pregnancy's insistence while fixing supper that it is necessary to lie down on the kitchen floor for a bit of a nap, or the prep for next morning's class frustrated by rubber-duckie baths and bedtime DeeDees and Lambies for toddlers. Between classes, it was possible to pick up the fifth grade son with the concussion from having his head bashed against a brick wall by a (female) classmate and get him to the doctor, and then to bring him to a discussion of the sword-play in Hamlet to keep him awake. On an academic schedule, kids' holidays and summer vacations often coincided at least partially with mine, and a camping trip outside Kalamazoo with a composition conference on the side could keep everyone busy and happy.

And, even more the intangibles pleasingly blended. I was fortunate a couple decades ago to read a little educational manifesto called *Paideia*, by the late University of Chicago philosopher Mortimer Adler. In passing, he mentioned that the three great "cooperative arts" were agriculture, medicine, and teaching—cooperative because they demand working *with* living material rather than imposing one's artistic will on inert substances. A very large light bulb flashed through my brain. Growing up on a farm

---

[13] "An Ex-con Icon," Washington Post Writers Group, 3 March 2005, http://www.workingforchange.com/printitem.cfm?itemid=18650

and in the woods, wanting to be a doctor, becoming instead an English professor, I had thought my life dismayingly disjointed and disconnected. And here I found that I had simply been migrating among the Great Cooperative Arts! Needless to say, I quickly added parenting to the list, and reveled in the unity of effort and sometimes achievement I felt between school and home.

Even more intangible, children, I think, give a sense of purpose to all kinds of life's activities which can otherwise seem depressingly repetitive or pointless, from cleaning toilets to earning a paycheck. When the academic world seemed too fraught with back biting, destructive gossip, unhealthy competitiveness, greedy cowardice, there was comparative innocence at home to soothe, mend, heal. I grew up painfully shy and basically lazy, things those who know me only now do not readily believe. Having kids gave me courage; doing something for someone else is a lot easier for the shy than doing it for oneself. And I was forced to set priorities, to multi-task, to the point where I got downright good at it (now that I don't have to do several things at once, I have totally lost the skill it seems). As for lazy, well I am returning surely if slowly to that early natural mode, too. Refuge can always, and for anyone, be found in reading, but refuge in action works for me with kids in a way that nothing else matches.

Many current articles on the opt-out revolution point out the great need for more flexibility in the business work schedule and work site, more tolerance of multiple roles in business culture, if talented women are to be kept working there. It seems to me, reading these laments, that much could be learned from candles and flashlights on campuses. For example, care for pre-schoolers or before- and after-school is often in close proximity to the working parent. (One of the things I am most proud of at UW-Whitewater is having been one of two women who got the still booming Child Care Center going way back when my youngest was a preschooler.) A lot of independence and responsibility for one's own classes makes it possible to achieve highly without being restricted to certain hours or places. It would seem to me that people in the business world trying to juggle families and work might well look to the academic not just for congenial work options, but for illumination adaptable to that business world.

It might be that things are moving the other way, though, into increasing darkness, in parts of the academic world. My nephew Randall Wedin tells me that women who like him have doctorates in chemistry are now often choosing industrial careers over academic ones since they find industry to be more flexible and accommodating to their needs. "Corporations tend to have well-defined benefit plans, specific rules on flex-time, internal systems for mentoring, clearly defined objectives/evaluations, better worker safety programs, diversity training, sensitivity to discrimination lawsuits," he writes, while "academic departments and universities are often still little fiefdoms where most of the rules are never written down and the unwritten rules are often stuck in the past." The universities may be learning from industry, though. He then refers to the recent highly-publicized announcement of the Stanford University Chemistry Department, that not just post-docs and faculty would be eligible for a "childbirth accommodation" policy, but now graduate students would as well. Geraldine L. Richmond, University of Oregon Chemistry Professor and chair of the Committee on the Advancement of Women Chemists, making note of the new Stanford policy, says that otherwise "when a woman is at the most vulnerable time in her personal career she has to go ask for time off or ask for an exceptional situation for herself." Whether other departments and other universities will follow Stanford is not yet known, but, Richmond notes, "when a few major universities stepped up and established policies for delaying the tenure clock for pregnant women faculty, other universities quickly followed suit. 'If you have a major department that's so highly regarded, like Stanford, there will be notice of this.'"[14]

This leads me to the present, to the retired state, to walls once again, walls of aging, walls of image, walls of self-image. We all face a certain amount of de-valuing, I think, in retirement. We are accustomed to a title which still carries some weight in our modern world—Dr. or Professor. We are accustomed to a certain amount of face-to-face deference from people dependent on us for grades. We are accustomed to feeling we are doing something important, that we are important in some way. We are accustomed to variety, if we want it, the chance to teach something new, to try a new method, to cooperate with people across disciplines or challenging personalities, to break new ground ourselves in our research, our writing.

---

[14]*Chemical & Engineering News: Weekly News Magazine of the American Chemical Society*, November 7, 2005, p. 8.

We are accustomed to having endings, closure—the end of the semester, the final grade list, the last version of a manuscript off to the publisher. We are accustomed to rewards—money sometimes, or a promotion, or a reduced course load, or getting to teach something one is passionate about, or an expense-paid trip to an exciting conference in a unique place, but more often a citation added to one's Curriculum Vitae, or the joy of seeing one's work in print, or a contact from a student years after he or she was in one's class. And we are accustomed to, addicted to, perhaps, regular new beginnings—the new faces, the new class list, the new semester, the new project, the new colleagues, the new challenge, the new chance.

Yes, we all face de-valuing with age, but women do more than men, I believe. A colleague tells of the respect paid her retired husband by a medical doctor because of what he had been, a professor, while the same regard was not paid to her, the wife, equally retired, professor for as much time. Used to being noticed in Heide Hall for my red spike heels and mini-skirts, I was shocked when I discovered that arthritic knees, black flats, and modest attire meant not just lack of notice but genuine invisibility. Truly, when I all-too-suddenly, it seemed, found myself fitting first the moniker "middle-aged" and then the technical orthopedic term, "old," eighteen-year-olds actually failed to see me when I met them in the hallway.

I know I have developed tricks for avoiding that blank, disinterested stare which follows the statement "I'm retired." My favorite is using the fact that I taught at Lund University in Sweden after leaving UW-Whitewater, and when I left Scandinavia I was asked to create and continue to teach an American Minority Writers course, which I have done several years since, interacting with Swedish students spread around the globe from my computer in the trees. So I experiment. "I'm retired," I say, and then as the automatic "oh, no brain" reaction starts creeping into the questioners eyes, I add, "from the University of Wisconsin," and as a bit of "or maybe . . ." replaces the disinterested stare, I position myself not only in the still-working world but in the wonderful world of the latest in technology: "Of course I teach an internet course for the University of Lund, Sweden." I smile a bit to myself as I see a smidgen of interest return. Cheating? Tricking people? Manipulative? Of course! But not lying, not deceiving—

and not caving in just yet to unhappy biases. The mind is the one thing that does not ever retire, I believe.

"Let me submit to art." I have not stopped learning, and I haven't stopped teaching, either, since I do some wonderful Community Education literature classes (wonderful equals no papers to grade). Why should my image from the world vary so much from my self-image, old though I rapidly be? I come at last to the other side of the benefit of having juggled roles all those years. It makes retirement easier to take. When the children were a refuge from the job, they gave me purpose. Now that they have taken flight from the nest they once needed, building stick by stick, straw by straw their own purposes, their own families and jobs, and don't require much from me, it is all those things from the job—the literature, the writing, even the teaching in new venues that give me my lift, that shed the light of day, of art, into the growing dark. Honesty directs me, though, to be more specific. In contrast to the days when my weekly TV viewing was limited to *Masterpiece Theatre* if I was lucky, I bask now in the regular glow of Badgers on Saturdays, the Packers on Sundays, *CSI Miami* on Mondays, *House* on Tuesdays, *ER* on Thursdays, *Numb3rs* on Fridays, *The Daily Show* and *Colbert Report* a glorious late four nights a week.

In his book based on his journals, *Taking Retirement: A Beginner's Diary*, academic Carl H. Klaus writes of those whose work is not "central" in life, "for someone whose life has followed such a pattern—and I suppose there must be millions of such people, especially women—retirement might well be a nonevent. Or better still a liberating experience."[15] This reveals a lot of misunderstanding of women and work outside the home, and even more of Klaus's female academic colleagues. His remark exhibits ignorance, really, based on "ignoring." But in a sense Klaus is happily correct more than he suspected, that a woman academic who has juggled career and family can indeed find retirement "liberating," not in spite of the juggling and all its pains and all its problems, but because of it, because it produces a rounder, more fully developed person who can revel in the drama of the day guilt free.

Walls and Candles, walls and candles. "Something there is that doesn't love a wall," ever, at any age. But "good fences make

---

[15] (Boston: Beacon Press, 1999) p. 72.

good neighbors," too, and it would be hard to live completely fence-free. And so, when boxed in, in the increasingly small spaces of aging, of image, of activity, may I still have the oomph to raise a hand and plop if not a tall candle, at least a little votive light, up there on the wall. When I taught in Sweden in the 1980s, I got very tired of negative people making use of my open door, the only welcoming weir in a hallway's torrent of complaint. So I put up a *New Yorker* cartoon with a good American allusion to "Don't Fence Me In." "The Range," said the sign backed by a wide horizon. "No discouraging words beyond this point." Not a bad image to carry onward and outward, inward, or upward further into retirement either.

Not a Leisured Renaissance

OCTOBER 19
5:02 a.m.

I am awake, as usual, and as usual this is my worry time. The bedroom is dark except for the nightlight that helps my husband find the bathroom since losing the sight in his left eye from the accident. The room is quiet except for the hum of the CPAP machine that he uses for his sleep apnea. The sleeping pill he takes at bedtime helps with his other sleep disorder. The doctors and I wonder how much these sleep disorders may have contributed to the fall off the horse in the first place.

I have been retired now for several months so this being awake long before I have to get up is not as annoying and exhausting as when I was teaching. Having a set time to worry was one of the tips I read about during the first year after my husband's brain injury. The idea is that you allow yourself this once-a-day space, then set it aside and get on with it. That's definitely easier said than done but I do try to follow the advice.

The health part is always a worry I visit each day. The accident was over nine years ago now—one-fourth of our marriage. Wayne, my husband, was fifty and I was forty-seven when the dream elk-hunting trip to Colorado with his two brothers turned into a nightmare from which we will never awake. The brain injury severely affected his short-term memory. He has numerous other health problems including diabetes, arthritis, and blood-clotting issues. He takes eleven medications, thirty-one pills each day that I oversee since he cannot do it for himself. The arthritis in his back has been the most urgent problem lately. Some days he can barely walk. I wonder how long I will be able to keep him in our home with me and how we will pay for his long-term care if it goes on for a long time. I know he is at great risk for Alzheimer's and he already takes one of the standard medications for that.

It is odd to have to be concerned with all this at the start of retirement—I am only fifty-six—but we lost those twenty-to-thirty "golden years" of middle-aged "empty nest" and "leisure renaissance" that are part of the normative life span, as I used to lecture about in my sociology classes. That is one of the difficult things now, watching our peers enjoy this stage of their lives. I've never been the jealous or envious type so I am happy to see friends enjoy the fruits of their labors. It's just that we also labored and our fruits rotted on the vine. Mostly I'm just bewildered.

We had planned to travel a lot in our retirement and a year before Wayne's accident we had bought a really neat time-share package. We may be able to use it a little bit domestically but international travel seems virtually impossible. Even domestically, I have to do all of the planning, arranging, packing, lifting, driving, etc. Anyway, a few weeks after we would return home Wayne would not remember much of the trip. Traveling has lost a lot of its appeal.

Some days I now get a few minutes to do something I enjoy—read, go for a walk, embroider, crochet. Since his accident and while still working, I never got those few minutes. I also had some bigger, personal plans for my retirement but they all crashed and burned nine years ago. I had hoped to write. I used to be a fairly good creative writer. Years of formulaic academic writing have probably taken their toll but I was hoping to resurrect my old talents; however, that would take big blocks of uninterrupted time and lots of psychic energy—neither of which I have now. I also wanted to audition for some community plays, acting being another small talent I used to enjoy. But when in a play, the show must be life's priority and I cannot give that kind of commitment.

Money is another worry. Wayne's medications cost about $2,000 a month—$24,000 a year. Thankfully, we have excellent health insurance—so far—and most of this is paid for. But premiums keep increasing and benefits keep decreasing. Besides the meds, there is monthly lab work, primary doctor visits, specialists, therapies. We have good investments but the stock market is so shaky. Social Security doesn't seem very secure the way the government plays political football with it. My pension is a fraction of what it should have been because of having to take early retirement to do care giving. I know this is common for women—I used to teach Women's Studies. How ironic to become your own lecture statistic!

My worry turns to the immediate—what today will be like. If it is a typical day, my husband will ask me approximately twenty-five times what day it is (I once counted). Twenty-five times a day, seven days a week, fifty-two weeks a year. This is only one of the many areas that require my patience. He repeats many of his thoughts and conversations many times a day, every day. Some days I can just keep repeating my part of the script and it just rolls off my back. Some days I want to run from the house screaming. I really, really miss having a *meaningful* conversation with him.

Wayne often likes to talk about the times before his accident. His long-term memory is quite good. He misses old friends. Many of our friends have remained in contact with us and I treasure that. But many have not and I know this is something that is typical with brain injury. Wayne is a very different person now and some people cannot make the transition. He is very hurt by what he feels is their indifference. Luckily his overall disposition is upbeat and he only broods over this for a short time each day.

I outline in my head the things I will need to do today— the usual housekeeping chores and general house maintenance. Since this is autumn there are all the leaves to rake and other getting-ready-for-winter projects. We have a big house and yard and have lived here for thirty-one years. It is getting to be too much for me to take care of all alone and I would like to sell it and move into a condo, though I know it would be hard to leave our home. I need to go through the basement and the garage and throw out most of what has accumulated over the years, but just the daily chores and crises keep me so busy and tired that I never get around to these big projects.

Today is Wednesday so Wayne will go to do his volunteer work at the local food pantry, as he also does on Fridays. On Tuesdays and Thursdays he volunteers at a local assisted living facility where he calls bingo for the residents. He has been doing this for seven years since he returned from his rehab. I hope he can continue doing this for a long time. He gets a real sense of purpose from these activities, some socialization, and a change of scene. And I get a few hours a week of much needed respite.

He too was an academic, teaching in the business department at the same university as I. A great teacher, well loved and respected, he was active in university governance. He was also active in the community and once spear-headed a $1 million dollar fund-raiser to bring artificial ice to our hockey arena. His skills for planning, organizing, and inspiring people were amazing. He has not taught since the accident and he misses it so much. Although the knowledge in his courses is still there in his head, his ability to plan and execute and his time management skills are gone. And of course the fatigue that is the legacy of brain injury makes all thinking exhausting. What a cruelty to him and to all the students he never got to teach.

Today as every day will be a battle over food with him. With diabetes, high cholesterol, high blood pressure, being about eighty pounds overweight, and unable to do much exercise, Wayne needs to limit his food intake. But eating is one of the few enjoyments he has left—surprising, considering he lost his sense of smell from the accident and that is so involved in the taste of food. I try to grocery shop when he is not along so we are not wrangling in the store in front of other people over buying doughnuts and cupcakes. We have no sweets in the house—ever. We usually cook meals together because he remembers how to cook but not to turn off the stove burners. He uses four times more dishes and utensils than needed so clean-up is a serious chore. (When he does the clean-up most things need to be redone). We do go out to eat quite often though, because, well, it is one of the few things Wayne can still enjoy. He can no longer drive, hunt, golf, or snowmobile. Even going to sports events is difficult for him because of climbing bleachers with arthritic joints and no depth perception due to the blind left eye. We can go to the movies if the characters are few and the plot not too complicated, otherwise he gets too confused. We go to bingo at the local Moose Lodge on Thursday nights and occasionally to the casino an hour away. I don't much care for either one, but incredibly Wayne's ability with numbers was not impaired by the brain injury. He usually wins at the blackjack table—go figure! I must do all the family finances, though, since he cannot handle the big picture and his hand-writing is almost illegible.

Sometime today we will play the card game "65" which Wayne loves and that I have become bored with after all these years. I play each day, of course, because I know these games are good for his mind and his self-esteem. His monthly poker group of neighborhood men recently disbanded after thirty years. He was devastated. Now he has no guy activity or time at all. I actually was as devastated as he was—another loss to absorb.

I will probably get a call from our daughter Heather today—I do most days since she and her family moved back to Wisconsin last year from the west coast. She is thirty and a stay-at-home mom with her two boys who are three and one-and-a-half. My grandsons are my pride and joy! Grandchildren are indeed the reward for not killing your teenagers! Wayne also loves them and being with them. He does things with them he never took time to do with our kids. He will sit for an hour (if *they* will sit that long) and draw, and color and do play-doh. For now, they are too young to realize that grandpa is any different from anyone else except that he uses a cane, and lots of people use canes.

When we are with the boys we both feel younger and happier, though they tire us out as all grandparents will admit. I have their pictures all over the house just to make us smile and I have even taken to wearing those silly holiday sweatshirts that older ladies wear because the boys like them so. I realize what a dotty old thing I'm becoming, but the grandsons are such an oasis in my life that I go blithely down that dotty old lane.

It was the day before Heather's twenty-first birthday when the accident occurred. She was starting her junior year in college. Our son, Heath, two years younger, was just starting his first year at West Point. I am so proud of the kids. Those first two years were rough with their dad in intensive care for weeks, hospitalized for months, and in and out of rehab centers. Lesser people would have quit school or turned down very bad roads. In my years of college teaching I saw many students give up or go bad for much lesser reasons. Our kids had to grow up overnight and I don't know how I would have gotten through the past nine years without their moral support and wonderful sense of humor.

Heather has a Master of Social Work degree with a concentration in gerontology, so she is my counselor as well as my daughter and friend. I can tell her the thoughts and fears and feelings I don't dare say to anyone else. On the other hand, I try to remember that my children for all intents and purposes lost their father nine years ago and they live in the same void and torment as I do, so I try not to burden them too much. My daughter says my life approach is called Defensive Pessimism, and that it is probably appropriate for the situation. I remember reading a novel in which the protagonist faced his problems with the motto, "Act positively, plan negatively, expect nothing." I find that it has become my motto also.

Heather has her own challenges, of course, and I remember vividly those days of 24/7 child care. It is not easy. We both would like to be able to be more help to each other but right now it is really difficult for one of us to take care of both Wayne and the two little boys alone for more than a day. We live about forty-five minutes away from each other so we try to get together at least once a week. Her husband, just like our son's wife, never knew my husband pre-injury. I don't know if that makes it easier or harder for them. They both are kind and accepting of the situation so we just go on as if all this were normal.

Our son and his wife live in Colorado and we hear from them about once a week. Heath was a captain in the army and has just finished his active duty requirement from West Point. Now he must serve three years of individual ready reserve which adds another worry, given the state of the world today. He has already served in Iraq for eleven months. He is a civil engineer and his unit was stationed north of Baghdad to rebuild schools. While he was there he could only call us occasionally and usually about 3 a.m. our time. That year I got almost no sleep at all. Two of his grandparents died during that time and he was not able to come home for either funeral. In fact, he only got four days of R&R out of Iraq in Qatar the whole time.

I cried the day Heath got his appointment to West Point— it was Christmas Eve, 1995. I came of age during the Vietnam War and have very strong feelings about what the military is sent to do and why. He himself is a "liberal" wanting to serve his country as well as wanting the West Point experience. He was graduated from there a little over a year when he got married and was only three days into his honeymoon when we were attacked on 9/11. When he and his wife returned three days later he took us to the same restaurant where his wedding reception had been and told me what to do about his burial should events go that way. We all sat crying in the same spot where less than a week earlier we had been laughing and celebrating. He is very happy to be in the civilian workforce now. I don't know if I could go through another year of him gone to a war zone, especially considering how I feel about this administration. My heart breaks for the families of those killed or wounded. I wonder how many soldiers have sustained brain injuries. They never tell us about them.

My worry turns to this country every day. Hillary Clinton says she lies awake at night worrying about it. Well, girlfriend, I be awake in the morning with the same worry. As I see it, we are in a combination McCarthy era (except that there's a supposed terrorist behind every tree instead of a Communist) and Vietnam (a war we can't win and should never have been in in the first place). I am disheartened by the political corruption of the current administration and mortified by the world's opinion of us. The only personal good for me from this horrible situation is that sometimes when I'm so down and tired and depressed with things at home, just thinking about how my wonderful native country has been ruined by these ideologues gets me so angry that the anger motivates me to go on. When I don't want to do my housework, I just think of this administration and I start cleaning with the vengeance I'd like to use to "clean house" in Washington: A grotesque irony of life is that this current national mess offers me respite from my personal mess! But in truth, I don't know if this country can ever recover from the ruin that has been wrought. When you have children and grandchildren you kind of assume that you will leave them a better world than what you had. I am so sorry and ashamed that this probably won't happen.

Oh—Wayne is starting to get out of bed, asking what day it is, what we will eat for meals, telling me which arthritic joints are most painful today. That means that I need to get up too, test his blood sugar, give him his morning meds, tackle the chore list.

OCTOBER 20
5:06 a.m.

I am awake, as usual, and as usual this is my worry time......

Patricia Zontelli

Loss

from *Red Cross Dog*

Digging up the bones. Reburying them.
Digging up the bones to see if they're still there.
Reburying them. Digging up the bones
to lick them one more time—licking them white
one more time under the white moon.
Burying them. Digging them up, just
to smell them, sniff any trace
of life there. Reburying them. Digging them up
to relieve the itch of my desire to see them,
to inhale their fading odor of blood, to
polish their hollows with my tongue,
turning them into something else, something
only I will recognize now. Burying them
in a place where even I can't find them.

Susan Thurin

An Ending

"You can come back now," I heard myself say to my husband, Erik. I was pacing the house, crying. The long dying was over, the memorial service done, the tombstone in place, bills paid. Though I was still waking often during the night, I felt more rested than I had in a long time. There were the fifty years of his journals to read, his books and photo collection to review, my lists of writing projects and household maintenance chores to tackle, yet I couldn't stop asking myself, "What do I do now?" I even caught myself thinking, just as I had fifteen years earlier after radical cancer surgery when chemotherapy left me feeling so bad, "Maybe I should just die too."

Long dyings, long endings, care giving, the feared retirement package, yet I'm lucky. In spite of everything, I'm reasonably happy most of the time. I have good health, wonderful relatives and friends, things to do, financial security, a nice home, and thanks to my heritage of generations of hard-working farm women, a genetic disposition to make the best of what comes one's way. "Life goes on," our aphoristic wisdom tells us, and it usually does in a predictable way—in fact, so predictably that Hospice provides detailed explanations of the grief and mourning process survivors will experience as well as that of the last months, weeks, and days of the dying.

But what is predictable to others seems unclear and confusing to those in the midst of it. Reviewing my journal during my husband's last months and my life since then, I am discomfited by my obtuseness to his deteriorating condition and my own unpreparedness for the succession of responses to care giving, death, and widowhood. Yet what to us was something so shattering and terrible that we couldn't believe it was really happening is something that must seem prosaic to others, the ordinary cycle of life.

Illness

(December 22, 2004) Cancer is a disease that just takes time. You live with it and try to ignore it until it prevents you from going about your life as usual.

(January 2005) It's my impression that the urologist did not mean to give Erik another lupron injection and prescribed Casodex only as a placebo because he thinks further treatment for the prostate cancer is hopeless. As an afterthought, he also sent us to a radiation oncologist who did not think radiation was called for but relented and gave us the opportunity to have that. Thousands and thousands of dollars of treatments—over $4k for radiation, $3k for lupron, nearly $3k for Casodex, and I don't believe the doctors think any of this will help at all, but Erik is hopeful and that is of great value. New experimental treatments might give Erik more viable time, but the oncologist said that Erik isn't a good candidate for them. His Parkinson's is advancing, he's seventy-five, and the side effects of aggressive cancer treatment are debilitating. In any case, Erik rebels against being a guinea pig.

(February 19, 2005) Erik's concerns about his health, at least those he talks about, are about seemingly inconsequential things, small skin eruptions, vague queasiness. The big thing, the cancer that is destroying his bones and ultimately will take his life, he never mentions. He apparently thinks that will take hold sometime in the future. Though he occasionally mentions the possibility of dying soon, it's clear that he doesn't really think that will happen. He has always believed he will die of a heart attack, like his father, but his heart is strong and always has been. If Erik is fearful of the course his cancer will take, he doesn't talk about it, and he certainly doesn't want to know much about it. He won't ask the doctors about it, preferring to take things as they come, not anticipate them. That may be best.

(May 5, 2005) Erik had his second Darbepoetin injection and will get one again in two weeks. The doctor said that the injections may not be able to do much good after that; the cancer may be too developed in another month. That would fit the timetable implied by the doctors.

Daily Life

(December 23, 2004) Yesterday I did my final grocery shopping for Christmas and today bought some wine, so for the next two days I'll concentrate on cooking and making a nice Christmas for us. It may be our last together. After all these years together, the prospect of being alone next year is hard to imagine.

(January 22, 2005) The Parkinson's disease makes it harder every day for Erik to perform his daily routine and he is also experiencing back pain in the morning and needs help getting out of bed. Getting legs into trousers, arms into sleeves, buttoning shirts, putting on socks and shoes, combing hair all require movements that are increasingly difficult and sometimes painful for him. Parkinson's is such a humiliating disease. Now Erik is at a stage when holding a fork or spoon is awkward, as if he has forgotten how it's done and he typically spills or drops food.

I can deal with helping Erik get dressed and eating, but his wrestling with the newspaper is getting on my nerves. The pages fall apart and he can't get them in order or folded. I used to get up earlier and read the paper before he got up but in the past few months I have been reading late at night so we get up at the same time and have breakfast together. This is more companionable, but . . .

After breakfast Erik falls asleep at the table. The kitchen chairs are comfortable and a good height for him, so this situation is okay. After sleeping in this position for about an hour, he works on his journal until lunch. After lunch he usually sleeps for an hour or more, spends time on his memoir and journals, and by 4:00 he is tired out. We watch TV news, eat dinner, doze, read and listen to music until we go to bed.

(Feb. 16, 2005) Today Erik seems better. The cancer and other complaints, the source of which is unclear, don't express themselves very acutely. Caring for Erik isn't time consuming but it is relentless and wears on me. I am sometimes short-tempered when he complains about anything I do that is not related to taking care of him or general upkeep chores. Then he says plaintively, "I'm a dying man," and I start to cry.

Writing

(Feb. 20, 2005) Last night I asked Erik about his journals, why he goes over the past. The answer was immediate, "To improve the style. One can always improve one's writing," he said, ever the English teacher and writer; my imagining other motives is wrong. As to whether I may read the journals, Erik always says no. He is quite pleasant about this. In the past, too, he was never very forthcoming when I brought up the journals, but it's clear he's leaving them to posterity, even though he sometimes says that he expects no one will read what he has written. I've told him I will try to edit them for publication after he's gone and he likes that idea. I hope it will be possible.

Waiting

(February 2005) I sit here staring at this title, unable to begin for a long time. Waiting. That seems to be one of my main activities in recent months. Every part of my day is subject to waiting. Erik's Parkinson's has made him slow. I always was quicker in any case, walked fast, ate fast, bustled about doing household chores, juggling work, cooking, housework, errands, taking care of things. Now I wait for Erik to get up in the morning. Some days I lie in bed listening to BBC or NPR on my Walkman for an hour or more as I wait for Erik to get up. Then I get breakfast ready while he showers and then I wait to help him get ready for the day. I've slowed down my own morning routine to accommodate him.

After breakfast Erik naps and I wait for him to awake before doing noisy household tasks. I wait for him to get ready for doctor appointments and help him with his coat. I wait as he struggles to get into the car, then help with the seat belt. I help him out of the car, wait for him in the doctor's office. I wait for him to finish meals. I wait for him to get ready for bed as he needs my help with his clothes and medications. I wait for him to settle down for the night, as shortly after falling asleep he is bothered by sleep disruptions, now usually groaning and moaning. Up to a few weeks ago he talked and shouted and often moved violently, thrashing around. The same pattern was repeated around five in the morning, but now this is replaced by the moaning and groaning, symptoms of Parkinson's or side effect of the Parkinson's medication.

I wait for the end of this waiting to start a new life. That sounds so heartless but it is true and I feel guilty about it. I'm not tied down every minute, by any means, yet . . . There is a short story, "To Room 19" by Doris Lessing, about a woman who goes mad owing to her sense of being tied down by tending to the needs of her children. I used to tell students the story was a parable about the traditional role of women, but I always found the character totally irritating for feeling unreasonably constrained by her few duties (she had servants, the children went to boarding school). She ends up spending endless hours in Room 19 of a seedy hotel, doing nothing in order to be free. I'm beginning to understand that character.

Loss of privacy, dignity

(March 8, 2005) Erik always guarded his privacy tenaciously. A few months ago I worried that this was a problem, that having someone take care of your daily needs, that telling others about your medical condition forfeited dignity and privacy, but now I don't care about it and I think Erik is beyond caring too. The daily needs are just there and wear one down. I complain a little to others and that makes me feel disloyal. Friends' queries are polite, but no one much understands the situation.

Memory

(February 5, 2005) I think about John Bayley's books about the rapid descent of his wife, Iris Murdoch, into the silences of Alzheimer's. A woman who had been a brilliant novelist and philosopher seemed to reverse the development process as she reverted to the mentality and dependencies of childhood and finally to the state when "Helplessness is all" (*Elegy for Iris*, p. 267). To an academic, Murdoch's loss of ability to verbalize thoughts, her loss of the ability to process information as an intelligent adult, seems most distressing. Any memory lapse of my own makes me fearful, and I worry that Erik is developing dementia. A man who spoke half a dozen languages fluently and who could read nearly as many more is losing facility with his immense vocabulary and often needs help to come up with a word or does the Alzheimer's thing of using a descriptive phrase as an alternative to a specific term.

(February 20, 2005) The decline in Erik's mental capacity is accelerating. He needs to verify the time when taking his pills even though they are in a box with sections clearly marked Morning, Noon, Evening, Night. He sometimes is confused about whether he is getting dressed for the day or undressed for the night. He confuses the hours, either adding or subtracting one. About past events his memory is selective. Some things he remembers well, but that may be only because he has written everything down and goes over his journals a lot. When I mention a past event he often says he doesn't remember it at all. The silver lining—he has forgotten that he doesn't like certain shirts, foods, and so on and this makes it easier to deal with him.

(April 25, 2005) Incoherencies are so amazing. About a week ago Erik was back in childhood, distressed about what to do with his school shoes. On Friday he was the worst he's ever been. He kept talking about carrying a heavy bucket, insisting we could try to carry it between us. Then he somehow associated this with baptism, and the whole sequence became an overt religious metaphor of the sort we would have enjoyed exploring in a class literary discussion.

Silences

(December 20, 2004) Erik has become so very passive. When he speaks he is clear, but increasingly he is simply silent. He is slow to respond and sometimes he thinks he has spoken though he has said nothing at all. He more and more lives within his own mind.

(February 26, 2005) I have tried to prod Erik to talk about his health and about, well, a sort of spiritual side to things, but he never responds. He understands what I say but often seems so in a fog that he can't think of what to say. He is not in bad spirits, most of the time. I don't understand his level of consciousness.

(April 2005) The silences on this journey are immense. Things we don't talk about:
Life after death.
What happens to me after Erik dies.
Our life before we met.

How we feel about me having to help him dress & feed him, wipe the drool from his beard.

Funeral, burial.

Erik sleeps a lot, wakes up briefly, says something coherent—or not—and falls back to sleep. In his clear-headed waking hours he sits at his computer. He won't talk about what he writes, but he sometimes is fretful about it. Maybe he is deleting passages that may be hurtful to others or just wants to get the record right.

Final Months

(April 3, 2005) On Thursday, Erik reached a critical point. He simply could not get to a standing position from the sofa with my help after several attempts, and so I called the paramedics. At the hospital they checked him for stroke, found his hemoglobin low and gave him a blood transfusion. The doctor seemed to want us to forgo this treatment, but I wanted it since it would improve Erik's condition. The doctor wanted Erik to stay overnight at the hospital to be assessed for nursing home or hospice care. I was shocked and did not feel ready for this—ending interventive treatment—and Erik couldn't understand the alternatives he was being offered. I—we—wanted us to carry on as best we could in our usual way until it became impossible to do so. *I didn't realize Erik was so near the end of his life, yet I knew this very well. How can one know yet not understand? In December the neurologist shook Erik's hand and wished him well with his prostate cancer in an apparent farewell gesture. I should have been more prepared for the end.*

(May 24, 2005) I see Erik getting steadily weaker, less able to walk and converse—his Parkinson's is worse, exacerbated by the cancer. Wouldn't it be enough to have only one of these horrible diseases? Perhaps in another month he will be bedridden most of the time. I doubt Erik will keep his August appointments, but the march of his cancer seems slow; he may make it to Christmas. He rarely complains of pain.

(May 25, 2005) The long, slow dying process is hard on both Erik and me. He is getting despondent, weaker, restless, losing his appetite, needs a lot of help with all physical activities. Last night he said he was getting tired of this and I can't blame him. It's no fun for either of us. We have always led a companion-

187

able, solitary life, reading and writing in our respective studies and spending the evenings reading and listening to music. Now it just seems solitary.

(May 30, 2005) How quickly events take over! Only two days after I wrote the previous entry, Erik collapsed. He had fallen as he was trying to get to the bathroom on his own. He said he didn't need my help, that he wanted some privacy, so I left him alone and then I heard a thump and found he had fallen again. I couldn't get him up and he had no strength to help himself. I asked our neighbor Kim to help us. During the night Erik got up three times and once even got to the bathroom without the walker, but the exertion was too much. He grew weaker Friday and by Saturday morning was unable to stand up. I managed to get him dressed and into the wheel chair. He had some yogurt and coffee and then wanted to go to bed. I called my sister Judy, a nurse, about what to do. *It seems so strange that I couldn't see this was the dreaded turning point we knew would come.* Because it upset Erik so much, I had delayed a visit by the Hospice social worker until this Tuesday.

The waiting seemed interminable at times but when the deterioration comes to this point, it seems sudden and hard and lonely.

Ending

I did what I promised I would never do, I put my husband in a nursing home. It seemed he might be able to regain the use of his legs enough so he could use a walker and wheel chair, but that never happened. When I told him his daughter and grandchildren would come to visit, he said, "Then I'm going to die." I couldn't think how to reassure him. He stopped eating more than a few mouthfuls and lost about twenty pounds in two weeks. Hades, he called it; I brought him home.

There were some tragi-comic moments in the last month. After visitors left, Erik would ask if they had paid for their own meal, and he worried about having money for tips. He attributed being in a strange room to being on a trip, in an accident, of being on our way to Smyrna. He wanted me to help him sneak out of the hospital, "then we can start our retirement." One day he accused me of trying to kill him. "What have I done?" I asked. "Do you deny you wrote that book?" he replied. "My book on Victorians in China?" I wondered to myself in disbelief.

Ten days before Erik died he called me to him and said "I'm dying." I held his hand and hugged him, and he apologized for past hurts. I couldn't stop crying. Then he rallied, ate a big breakfast, and resumed his confused ramblings. We listened to our collection of Haydn and Mozart and of Evert Taube, the old Swedish songs Erik loved.

My older brother Clem died suddenly of a heart attack on June thirtieth. Erik, as one does when learning that an age-mate has died, felt some satisfaction in surviving still and lived four days more. Morphine numbed his pain.

Death, when it came just after noon on the fourth of July, was quiet, a faint gasping for air. I felt stunned, closed his eyes, bathed him as best I could, called the Hospice nurse, watched the undertaker zip him into a body bag. For the next week I kept hearing Erik breathe, calling me to help him.

Notes on Contributors

Richard Beckham served as English Department chair at the University of Wisconsin-River Falls for nine years and taught British Literature and Humanities courses for many more. In retirement he hones his skills as a photographer and travels widely and frequently. He has made numerous visits to the United Kingdom and was resident lecturer at University College of St. Martin's in Lancaster in 1995.

Sue Bridwell Beckham, is a southerner by birth and northerner in translation. Her specialty is Southern Material Culture with emphasis on the Depression. She is the author of *Southern Depression Post Office Murals: A Gentle Reconstruction* (LSU Press), articles on the cultural implications of the Southern front porch, and Southern artists and art works. With degrees in English and American Studies, Sue taught writing courses, cultural studies of American cinema, best sellers and detective fiction in the English Department at the University of Wisconsin-Stout.

Gene Bloedorn tries to tell a story as an artist by using carefully rendered images. It was his habit as an artist to write notes, descriptive sentences, in the margins of his drawings to help him understand what he was trying to say. One day, pencil in hand, he discovered that he was giving more time and more thought to the writing in the margins than to the drawing itself. Now he just writes instead of draws. He is retired from the Art Department at the University of Wisconsin-Stout.

Jared Brown, was the Director of the School of Theatre Arts at Illinois Wesleyan University. He is the author of *Zero Mostel: A Biography*, *The Fabulous Lunts* (winner of the 1987 Barnard Hewitt Award for Outstanding Book on Theatre), *Theater in America During the Revolution*, *Alan J. Pakula: His Films and His Plays*, and *Moss Hart, A Prince of the Theater*. He has also written numerous plays and essays and has directed approximately one hundred productions. In 1997, he was the recipient of the DuPont Award for Teaching Excellence. He and his wife Judy live in Bloomington, Illinois.

Judy Brown now spends her days as Executive Director of the Illinois Theatre Consortium, a production company overseeing three theatres. She served as director, writer and actor for the Illinois Voices Theatre, has performed in Illinois Wesleyan University's summer theatre and with Heartland Theatre. She also tours her one-woman show regionally.

Carol Dolphin, Communication Arts/Theater Department, University of Wisconsin Colleges, Waukesha campus spends her joyful retirement as a world traveler, community volunteer, and occasional actor.

James Eggert taught Economics for thirty-one years at the University of Wisconsin-Stout. His articles and essays have appeared in *The Empty Vessel*, *The Progressive Populist*, *Religious Humanism*, and *The Washington Post*. His books include *What Is Economics?*, *Invitation to Economics*, *Investigating Microeconomics*, *Meadowlark Economics*, *Low-Cost Earth Shelters*, *Song of the Meadowlark*, and *The Wonder of the Tao*. Eggert's degrees are from Lawrence University and Michigan State University. He served two years in the Peace Corps (Kenya, 1964-66).

Richard Gardner spent his childhood helping build the family hobby farm in Orange County, California. He majored in Creative Writing at Stanford, attended the University of Iowa Writer's Workshop, did his doctoral work at the University of California at Irvine, and taught in the English Department at the University of

Wisconsin-Stout for thirty-seven years. He has published in all genres of creative writing as well as essays linking tourism and literature, on the use of stereotypes, and teaching. He served as assistant editor for *Annals of Tourism Research*, and self-publishes a monthly humorous newsletter *Flea Bytes*.

Margaret T. Gordon's administrative career began at Northwestern University where she directed the Institute for Policy Research and taught at the Medill School of Journalism. In 1988 she joined the University of Washington as Dean of the Evans School of Public Affairs, a position she held for ten years. Subsequently, she taught and collaborated on research evaluating the impacts of the Gates Foundation's gift of 50,000 computers to over 11,000 public libraries. She retired in June, 2004.

Liina Keerdoja is a trained librarian (MSLS, Columbia University, 1967) with a thirty-seven year career at the Library of Congress and the State Department. Before becoming a librarian she was a French major, German minor at Indiana University (BA, 1964; Phi Beta Kappa), and after that, a graduate student in Uralic Studies (MA, 1966). She also has a certificate in French-English translation (Georgetown University, 1970) and has taught cataloging. A native Estonian (and WWII refugee), she has done some Estonian-English, English-Estonian translating. She enjoys the performing arts, and likes to read, travel, and tap dance.

David McCordick is the editor of *Scottish Literature: An Anthology*, vols. 1 & 2 published by Peter Lang, vol. 3 by the Scottish Cultural Press of Edinburgh, thanks in part to a grant from the Scottish Arts Council. McCordick also edited *The Civil War Letters (1862-1865) of Private Kaufmann, Henry: The Harmony Boys Are All Well*. Both a passionate theatergoer and playwright, McCordick's plays have been staged at university and professional theaters. He is enjoying his retirement from the English Department at the University of Wisconsin-Stout by traveling the world.

Robert Meier taught English at the University of Wisconsin-Stout, has degrees from Brown University and the University of Arizona, and is spending his retirement as a professional photographer. His work has appeared in two dozen solo and group exhibitions and is in several permanent collections in Minnesota and Wisconsin. He received a New Partnership Fund Grant for the creation of the exhibit "U B ME." His photos have appeared in such magazines as *Architecture Minnesota* and *The New Yorker.*

Sheri Nero taught in the Social Science Department at the University of Wisconsin-Stout. She has a B.A. and M.A. in Sociology from the University of Illinois-Chicago and a Ph.D. in Education from the University of Minnesota. She retired in 2005 after twenty-seven years in the University of Wisconsin System. While at UW-Stout she was director of the Women's Studies Program for five years and received the Outstanding Teaching Award in 1994. She resides in Menomonie, Wisconsin with her husband.

William O'Neill worked as a technical writer for about ten years before becoming an English professor at the University of Wisconsin-Stout. He directed the Wisconsin in Scotland program, a study-abroad program for students of the western Wisconsin universities, for a year before retiring in 2001. He lives in Menomonie with his wife Jeanette. They have two grown children, a veterinarian daughter, Siobhan, and a film-maker son, Colin. O'Neill's articles have appeared in *Descant, Journal of Twentieth Century Literature, Etudes Irlandaise* and *The Progressive Populist.*

Sudershan Perusek earned her Ph.D. at Kent State University, taught there and at Akron University and the College of Medicine in Rootstown, Ohio before joining the English Department, University of Wisconsin-Stout. Her publications include essays in the *Cream City Review, The Center of the Web: Women and Solitude* and *The Family Track.* She was editor of *Kaleidoscope: Magazine of Literature, Art, and Disability* from 1985-2001. Her retirement has given her time to put to use her talents in the kitchen by offering classes in cooking at the local Co-Op, and to coax her orchids to bloom.

Leland L. Nicholls served the Department of Hospitality and Tourism, University of Wisconsin-Stout as program director and department chair. He was also a director of the Wisconsin Institute for Service Excellence International, and was on the Board of External Examiners at Ngee Ann Polytechnic University in Singapore. He earned a doctorate from the University of Tennessee and completed post-doc programs at the Harvard School of Business, the University of Wisconsin-Madison, the Disney Institute, and the Ritz Carlton Leadership Center. He is a resource editor of *The Journal of Hospitality Human Resources* and has published in professional, academic and trade journals.

Mary E. Thompson, Ph.D., Department of Human Development and Family Studies at the University of Wisconsin-Stout, came to the University of Wisconsin-Stout to be Assistant Dean of the School of Home Economics in 1975. She held both teaching and administrative positions until retiring in July 2004. She most enjoyed the challenge of facilitating the conversation between faculty, staff and administrators.

Erik Thurin taught in the English Department at the University of Wisconsin-Stout. A native of Sweden, Thurin was a philologist by both inclination and education. He taught French, Latin and Greek in Sweden, then added to his considerable academic record there, a Ph.D. in American literature at the University of Minnesota. He is the author of *Emerson Priest of Pan*, *Whitman between Impressionism and Expressionism*, *The Humanization of Willa Cather*, and *The American Discovery of the Norse*. He spent his retirement doing what he most loved: reading, writing, traveling, and learning a new language, biblical Hebrew.

Susan Schoenbauer Thurin taught English for thirty-five years at the University of Wisconsin-Stout. She also was a Peace Corps Volunteer in Liberia, taught in a boys' prep school in England and in universities in China and Sweden. Her publications include *Victorian Travelers and the Opening of China, 1842-1907*; *Nineteenth-Century Travels, 1835-1910: The Far East*; and numerous essays on Victorian novels and travel literature. Nowadays she is one of those busier-than-ever retirees.

Carolyn Wedin taught for thirty years in Languages and Literature at the University of Wisconsin-Whitewater with year-long appointments in UW-System Administration; the University of Gothenburg, Sweden; the University of Lund, Sweden; and Fulbrights at the University of Silesia in Poland and the Norwegian Royal Ministry of Education. She has published scholarly works on women's and African American literature and history, general audience radio commentaries, and other writing. She is married, with three grown children and four grandchildren.

Patricia Zontelli's second collection of poetry, *Red Cross Dog*, was the winner of the Headland Poetry Competition. Her poems have appeared in *Beloit Poetry Review, Calyx, Connecticut Poetry Review, Gettysburg Review, Kansas Quarterly, Los Angeles Times, Spoon River Poetry Review* and many UK journals. She was awarded a Bush Artist Fellowship, Wisconsin Arts Board grant and was a winner of the Lake Superior Regional Writers Competition and Loft Mentor Series. She taught in the Art Department, University of Wisconsin-Stout, and now divides her time between London, England and Menomonie, Wisconsin with her husband Charles Wimmer. She never refers to herself as retired.